Table of Contents

Introduction: Navigating Modern Love 5
Contemporary Dynamics of Love and Relationships 5
Changing Perspectives on Valentine's Day Today 8
Technology's Impact on Modern Expressions of Love 11

Chapter 1: Technological Influences on Modern Romance 15
The Role of Dating Apps in Contemporary Love 15
Online Communication and Virtual Connections 19
Social Media's Impact on Relationship Dynamics 24
Tech Innovations Redefining Modern Dating 30

Chapter 2: Changing Dynamics of Romantic Relationships 35
Evolving Notions of Love and Commitment 35
Shifting Gender Roles in Modern Relationships 41
Impact of Individualism on Partnership 48
Diversity in Relationship Structures Today 54

Chapter 3: Celebrity Influence on Valentine's Day Trends 60
Pop Culture Icons Shaping Romantic Ideals 60
Influence of Celebrity Relationships on Public Perceptions ... 66
Celebrity-Endorsed Brands in the Love Industry 72
Impact of Social Media on Celebrity Romance 77

Chapter 4: Virtual Celebrations and Long-Distance Love 84
Navigating Love Across Time Zones 84
Virtual Celebrations and Shared Online Experiences 90
Challenges and Joys of Long-Distance Relationships 96
Technology's Role in Sustaining Long-Distance Love 102

Chapter 5: The Psychology of Love Today 108

Modern Psychosocial Perspectives on Love 108
Impact of Social Media on Self-Perception in Relationships 114
Digital Communication and Emotional Intimacy 119
Online Dating and its Psychological Effects 125
Chapter 6: Love in the Age of Globalization **132**
Cross-Cultural Relationships and International Love 132
Global Perspectives on Love and Marriage 139
Challenges and Advantages of Globalized Love 145
The Role of Travel in Modern Love Stories 154
Chapter 7: Future Trends in Love and Relationships
.... **160**
Emerging Trends in Love and Partnership 160
Technology's Future Impact on Love 166
Changing Views on Marriage and Commitment 172
Anticipating the Evolution of Modern Love 178
Conclusion: Love in the 21st Century **184**
Reflecting on Contemporary Expressions of Love 184
Navigating the Complexities of Modern Relationships 190
Embracing the Fluidity and Diversity of Love Today 195
Glossary **201**
Potential References **204**

Copyright © 2024 by Blaze X. Maverick (Author)
All rights reserved. This book or any portion thereof may not be reproduced or used in any manner whatsoever without the express written permission of the publisher except for the use of brief quotations in a book review.

This book is copyright protected. This is only for personal use. You cannot amend, distributor, sell, use, quote or paraphrase any part or the content within this book without the consent of the author.

Please note the information contained within this document is for educational and entertainment purposes only. Every attempt has been made to provide accurate, up to date and reliable complete information. No warranties of any kind are expressed or implied. Readers acknowledge that the author is not engaging in the rendering of legal, financial, medical or professional advice. The content of this book has been derived from various sources. Please consult a licensed professional before attempting any techniques outlined in this book.

By reading this document, the readers agree that under no circumstances are the author responsible for any losses, direct or indirect, which are incurred as a result of the use of information contained within this document, including but not limited to errors, omissions or inaccuracies.

Thank you very much for reading this book.

Title: Navigating Modern Love
Subtitle: Technological Influences on Modern Romance

Series: Eternal Valentine: Stories of Enduring Love: From Ancient Traditions to Modern Expressions
Author: Blaze X. Maverick

Introduction: Navigating Modern Love
Contemporary Dynamics of Love and Relationships

In the ever-evolving landscape of romance, where traditional notions of love find themselves entwined with the advancements of technology, the dynamics of modern love and relationships are undergoing a profound transformation. As we embark on this exploration, we delve into the heart of contemporary expressions of love, observing the intricate interplay between age-old emotions and the influence of the digital era. This introduction sets the stage for a journey through the multifaceted realms of modern romance.

In the 21st century, love has transcended its conventional boundaries, adapting to the dynamic societal shifts that define our era. The conventional trajectory of courtship and commitment has been redefined, giving rise to a diverse spectrum of relationships. As we navigate the complex web of modern love, it becomes apparent that these dynamics are shaped by a myriad of factors, with technology standing as a central force.

The Interplay of Tradition and Progress: Contemporary love is a fusion of tradition and progress, a delicate dance between the timeless essence of human connection and the rapid pace of technological innovation. While the core emotions of love remain constant, the methods of expression and the avenues for connection have undergone a radical metamorphosis. Technology has become an inseparable companion on the journey of modern love, influencing how we meet, communicate, and sustain relationships.

Shifting Landscape of Commitment: The traditional markers of commitment, such as marriage, have seen a perceptible shift in significance. Modern relationships often navigate the terrain of commitment without the need for formal unions. As societal norms transform, the emphasis on personal growth and individual fulfillment intertwines with the evolving definition of commitment. The role of technology in facilitating and challenging these commitments becomes a key focal point in understanding the contemporary dynamics of love.

Fluidity in Relationship Structures: In contrast to the rigid structures of relationships in the past, the 21st century witnesses a remarkable fluidity in how individuals define their partnerships. Non-traditional relationships, open arrangements, and polyamory are gaining acceptance, challenging conventional norms. This fluidity allows individuals to tailor their relationships to suit their unique needs, and technology plays a pivotal role in connecting like-minded individuals across the globe.

The Influence of Digital Communication: Communication, the lifeblood of any relationship, undergoes a revolution in the age of smartphones and social media. Text messages, emojis, and instant communication platforms shape the way couples express affection, share experiences, and navigate challenges. The immediacy of digital communication creates both opportunities for connection and potential pitfalls, as the boundaries between the virtual and the real blur.

Impact of Social Media on Relationship Perception: Social media platforms serve as both a canvas and a mirror for modern relationships. Couples showcase their love through carefully curated posts, shaping external perceptions and internal expectations. The pressure to conform to curated ideals of happiness, fueled by influencers and celebrities, introduces a layer of complexity to the dynamics of modern love.

As we navigate the contemporary dynamics of love and relationships, it becomes evident that the landscape is as diverse as the individuals who traverse it. In the chapters that follow, we will dissect these dynamics further, examining the intricate interplay between technology, societal shifts, and the timeless essence of love in the 21st century. Join us on this journey through the multifaceted realms of modern romance, where tradition and innovation coalesce in the intricate dance of human connection.

Changing Perspectives on Valentine's Day Today

In the enchanting tapestry of modern romance, where the threads of tradition weave seamlessly with the strands of innovation, our exploration delves deeper into the intricate nuances that define love in the 21st century. As we navigate the evolving landscapes of contemporary relationships, an integral facet that demands our attention is the shifting perspective on a day that epitomizes love and affection – Valentine's Day.

Once confined to the exchange of handwritten notes and tokens of affection, Valentine's Day has metamorphosed over the years, reflecting the changing dynamics of love in our society. Traditionally associated with expressions of romantic love, this day has expanded its boundaries to encompass a broader spectrum of relationships, transcending the conventional norms that once defined it.

From Romantic Tradition to Inclusive Celebration: Valentine's Day, steeped in centuries of romantic tradition, has undergone a contemporary makeover. What was once solely a celebration of romantic love has evolved into a more inclusive observance, recognizing and honoring various forms of affectionate connections. Friends, family, and self-love now share the stage, as society embraces a more expansive definition of love.

The rise of Galentine's Day, a day dedicated to celebrating female friendships, and Palentine's Day, emphasizing camaraderie among friends, exemplifies this shift. The contemporary perspective on Valentine's Day acknowledges that love, in all its forms, is worthy of celebration. Whether it be the love between partners, friends, or oneself, the day has become a canvas for diverse expressions of affection.

Challenges to Conventional Notions of Love: Modern perspectives on love challenge the conventional narrative associated with Valentine's Day. The emphasis on individualism and self-love questions the societal expectation that one's happiness should be contingent on a romantic partner. The celebration of self-love encourages individuals to indulge in acts of kindness and appreciation for themselves on Valentine's Day, fostering a positive and empowering outlook.

Moreover, the evolving dynamics of romantic relationships contribute to a reevaluation of the significance attached to grand gestures on Valentine's Day. The modern couple may prioritize shared experiences, quality time, and authentic connection over traditional symbols of love, such as elaborate gifts or extravagant dinners. The changing nature of relationships influences how individuals approach and perceive Valentine's Day, emphasizing the importance of meaningful gestures over societal expectations.

Commercialization and Alternative Celebrations: The commercialization of Valentine's Day, with its inundation of heart-shaped products and marketing campaigns, has prompted a countercultural response. Some individuals reject the commodification of love and choose alternative, less materialistic ways to celebrate. Handmade gifts, experiential dates, and acts of service gain prominence as people seek to infuse authenticity into their expressions of love.

Anti-Valentine's Day sentiments have also emerged, with some individuals actively opposing the perceived pressure and consumerism associated with the holiday. This countermovement embraces the freedom to express love on one's own terms, detached from societal expectations and commercial influences.

Technology's Role in Redefining Romantic Gestures: The digital age has left an indelible mark on how Valentine's Day is celebrated. The exchange of virtual cards, online messages, and social media expressions of love has become a commonplace way to connect on this special day. Technology facilitates long-distance celebrations, enabling couples separated by geographical distances to share moments of intimacy through video calls, virtual experiences, and shared online spaces.

Social media platforms, in particular, have become a stage for public displays of affection, where couples showcase their love through curated posts and stories. This digital manifestation of love adds a layer of complexity to Valentine's Day, as individuals navigate the balance between authenticity and the desire to present an idealized version of their relationships.

As we navigate the changing perspectives on Valentine's Day in the 21st century, it becomes apparent that the day's essence has evolved beyond traditional romantic expressions. It now serves as a canvas for diverse forms of love and a reflection of the societal shifts influencing modern relationships. In the following chapters, we will further explore how technology intertwines with this evolving narrative, shaping the ways in which love is expressed and celebrated in the digital age. Join us on this journey through the nuanced tapestry of modern love, where Valentine's Day stands as both a symbol and a reflection of the diverse, ever-changing landscapes of affection and connection.

Technology's Impact on Modern Expressions of Love

As we embark on a journey through the intricate tapestry of modern romance, our exploration deepens into the profound influence of technology on the very essence of love. In this chapter, we navigate the ever-evolving landscape of modern expressions of love, where the digital age intertwines with age-old emotions, reshaping the way we communicate, connect, and express affection.

In the 21st century, technology has become an integral companion on the journey of love, influencing how individuals express their deepest emotions and navigate the complex terrain of modern relationships. From the early stages of courtship to the sustained connections in long-term partnerships, technology's impact is multifaceted, transforming the very language of love.

Digital Courtship: The onset of a modern love story often begins in the digital realm, where dating apps have emerged as the contemporary matchmakers of our time. These platforms, with their algorithms and swiping mechanics, have redefined how individuals initiate connections. The convenience and accessibility offered by dating apps have democratized the process of finding love, allowing people to transcend geographical barriers and connect with potential partners they might not encounter in their everyday lives.

However, the digital courtship landscape comes with its own set of challenges. The paradox of choice, where an abundance of options can lead to decision paralysis, and the commodification of relationships are among the complexities individuals navigate in the pursuit of love. As we delve into the impact of dating apps on modern romance, we uncover the ways in which technology shapes the initial stages of connection, influencing preferences, expectations, and the dynamics of attraction.

Online Communication and the Language of Love: Communication, the cornerstone of any relationship, undergoes a metamorphosis in the digital age. Text messages, emojis, and multimedia exchanges have become the primary means through which couples express affection, share experiences, and maintain a sense of closeness. The asynchronous nature of digital communication allows for constant connection, fostering a sense of intimacy even in the absence of physical proximity.

Yet, as the digital language of love evolves, it brings forth both opportunities and challenges. The immediacy of messaging can enhance connection, but it also introduces the potential for misunderstandings. The absence of non-verbal cues, such as tone and body language, in digital exchanges adds layers of complexity to the interpretation of messages. As we navigate the impact of online communication on modern expressions of love, we explore the delicate balance between the convenience of constant connection and the nuances lost in the absence of face-to-face interaction.

Social Media's Role in Relationship Narratives: Social media platforms serve as a canvas for individuals to paint the portrait of their relationships, showcasing moments of joy, shared experiences, and expressions of love. Couples curate their digital personas, constructing a narrative that reflects their idealized version of love. From relationship status updates to anniversary posts, social media becomes a tool for public declarations of affection, shaping external perceptions and internal dynamics.

However, the intersection of social media and modern love introduces complexities. The pressure to conform to curated ideals of happiness, fueled by influencers and celebrities, can impact individuals' self-esteem and contribute to unrealistic expectations. Additionally, the public nature of these displays raises questions about the authenticity of the love portrayed online. In navigating the impact of social media on modern expressions of love, we dissect the interplay between curated narratives and the authentic, often messy, reality of relationships.

Tech Innovations Redefining Romantic Gestures: In the realm of modern love, technology extends beyond facilitating connections; it actively shapes the way couples express affection. From virtual reality date nights to the use of love-themed apps, technology offers innovative avenues for couples to deepen their connection and create shared experiences. The digital landscape becomes a playground for romantic gestures, where couples can transcend physical limitations to express love in novel ways.

However, the integration of technology into romantic gestures raises questions about the authenticity of these experiences. Can a virtual date truly capture the essence of an in-person encounter? How do technological innovations impact the sincerity of romantic expressions? In exploring the role of tech innovations in redefining modern romantic gestures, we unravel the intricate balance between the convenience of digital experiences and the timeless authenticity of genuine, physical expressions of love.

As we navigate the impact of technology on modern expressions of love, it becomes clear that the digital age has reshaped not only how we find love but also how we articulate and sustain it. In the chapters that follow, we will delve deeper into specific facets of this transformation, examining the nuances of digital courtship, online communication, social media's influence, and the innovative ways in which technology becomes a conduit for expressions of love. Join us on this exploration of the intricate dance between love and technology, where the language of the heart finds new expressions in the digital echoes of the 21st century.

Chapter 1: Technological Influences on Modern Romance

The Role of Dating Apps in Contemporary Love

In the digital era, where love and technology intersect in unprecedented ways, our exploration begins with an in-depth analysis of the role of dating apps in shaping the landscape of contemporary love. From the initial spark of connection to the complexities of virtual courtship, dating apps have emerged as the architects of modern romance, reshaping how individuals meet, connect, and navigate the intricate dance of relationships.

In the not-so-distant past, the quest for love often involved chance encounters, mutual connections, or the traditional matchmaking orchestrated by friends and family. However, the 21st century ushered in a revolutionary change with the advent of dating apps, transforming the dynamics of courtship and challenging established norms in the pursuit of love.

Democratizing the Search for Love: Dating apps have democratized the process of finding love, breaking down geographical barriers and providing individuals with a vast pool of potential partners at their fingertips. The algorithms powering these platforms analyze user preferences, interests, and behaviors to curate a selection of potential matches. This algorithmic approach aims to enhance compatibility and streamline the dating process, allowing users to explore connections beyond the constraints of physical proximity.

The democratization of the search for love, while offering unprecedented access to potential partners, also raises questions about the impact of choice overload. With a seemingly infinite array of options, individuals may grapple with decision paralysis, making it challenging to navigate the complexities of modern dating. As we delve into the role of dating apps, we navigate the delicate balance between choice and decision-making in the pursuit of meaningful connections.

Virtual First Impressions: In the realm of contemporary love, the first impression often unfolds in the digital realm. Profile pictures, witty bios, and shared interests become the initial markers of attraction, shaping perceptions before the first conversation even takes place. Dating apps have introduced a visual and curated element to first impressions, where individuals craft online personas to convey specific aspects of their personalities.

However, this curated approach to self-presentation raises questions about authenticity. How accurately do dating app profiles reflect the complexities of an individual's character? How does the visual nature of these platforms influence attraction and compatibility? As we explore the virtual landscape of first impressions, we unravel the nuances of self-presentation in the digital age and its impact on the development of modern romantic connections.

Challenges of Digital Introductions: While dating apps offer a convenient and accessible platform to initiate connections, they also present unique challenges in the realm of digital introductions. The absence of non-verbal cues, such as body language and tone of voice, complicates the interpretation of messages and the development of genuine connection. Navigating the balance between digital communication and face-to-face interaction becomes a crucial aspect of modern courtship.

Moreover, the potential for misrepresentation on dating apps raises concerns about trust and authenticity. Catfishing, the practice of creating fake identities, and the use of heavily edited photos challenge the integrity of the digital dating landscape. As we delve into the challenges of digital introductions, we examine the ways in which technology both facilitates and complicates the process of getting to know someone in the quest for love.

Changing Dynamics of the First Date: The digital revolution extends beyond the initial stages of connection to reshape the dynamics of the first date. Dating apps often facilitate a level of pre-date interaction through messaging, voice calls, or video chats, altering the traditional paradigm of meeting someone for the first time in person. This shift introduces a layer of familiarity before the physical encounter, influencing the dynamics of that crucial first date.

The incorporation of technology in the early stages of courtship raises intriguing questions about the evolution of romantic rituals. How do digital interactions impact the chemistry and authenticity of the first date? How does the integration of technology influence individuals' expectations and experiences during this pivotal moment in the progression of a relationship? As we explore the changing dynamics of the first date in the digital age, we unravel the ways in which technology shapes the trajectory of modern romance.

Impact on Relationship Expectations: Dating apps not only influence how individuals meet but also shape their expectations regarding relationships. The swiping culture, where users make rapid decisions based on limited information, can contribute to a disposable mentality, where individuals may view relationships as easily replaceable commodities. The instant gratification provided by dating apps can impact the patience and commitment individuals are willing to invest in the process of building a meaningful connection.

As we navigate the impact of dating apps on relationship expectations, we delve into the nuances of balancing the efficiency of modern digital dating with the depth required for authentic and lasting connections. How do dating apps influence individuals' perceptions of commitment, and how does this shape the trajectory of relationships in the 21st century?

In examining the role of dating apps in contemporary love, it becomes evident that these digital platforms have not only revolutionized the way individuals connect but have also introduced a set of complexities and challenges. From the democratization of the search for love to the changing dynamics of the first date, the influence of dating apps on modern romance is profound. Join us as we unravel the intricacies of virtual courtship and explore the impact of technology on the foundations of 21st-century love.

Online Communication and Virtual Connections

In the intricate dance of modern romance, the rhythm of connection is increasingly orchestrated by the cadence of online communication and virtual connections. As we navigate the profound influence of technology on the intricate fabric of contemporary love, this chapter unfolds the layers of how digital interactions shape the way individuals communicate, express affection, and forge meaningful connections in the digital age.

The Evolution of Digital Dialogue: The advent of the internet brought forth a transformative shift in how individuals communicate, transcending the constraints of time and space. Online communication, once confined to the realm of emails and instant messaging, has evolved into a multifaceted landscape that plays a pivotal role in the narrative of modern romance. Social media platforms, messaging apps, and dating websites have become conduits for expressing affection, sharing experiences, and sustaining connections in the digital realm.

The evolution of digital dialogue introduces both opportunities and challenges. The immediacy and accessibility of online communication allow for constant connection, fostering a sense of intimacy even in the absence of physical proximity. However, the absence of non-verbal cues in digital exchanges adds layers of complexity, as individuals navigate the nuances of expression without the benefit of facial expressions, gestures, or tone of voice.

The Language of Emoji and Digital Expression: In the realm of online communication, the language of love has expanded to include a vibrant array of emojis and digital expressions. These small, colorful symbols transcend linguistic barriers, allowing individuals to convey emotions, affection, and nuances in a concise and visually engaging manner. From heart emojis to GIFs expressing complex emotions, the digital lexicon has become a canvas for articulating the subtleties of modern romance.

Yet, the reliance on emojis and digital expressions raises questions about the potential for misinterpretation. How accurately do these symbols convey the depth and sincerity of emotions? Do they enhance or hinder the clarity of communication in the context of romantic relationships? As we explore the language of emoji and digital expression, we unravel the intricate interplay between visual communication and the complexities of conveying emotions in the digital realm.

Virtual Intimacy and Emotional Connection: The digital age has redefined the concept of intimacy, introducing the notion of virtual closeness. Video calls, voice messages, and shared digital spaces enable couples to bridge geographical distances and maintain a sense of connection in the absence of physical presence. Virtual intimacy transcends traditional boundaries, allowing partners to share moments, experiences, and even intimate conversations in real-time.

However, the question of authenticity in virtual intimacy lingers. Can a screen truly capture the essence of a person? How does the absence of physical proximity impact the depth of emotional connection in virtual relationships? As we delve into the realm of virtual intimacy, we explore the ways in which technology facilitates emotional closeness and the challenges associated with sustaining genuine connection in the digital space.

Challenges of Digital Miscommunication: While online communication provides a platform for constant connection, it also introduces the potential for miscommunication. The lack of non-verbal cues in digital exchanges can lead to misunderstandings, as the nuances of tone, intent, and emotion may be lost in translation. Text messages, often stripped of context, can be subject to varying interpretations, contributing to communication breakdowns in romantic relationships.

Navigating the challenges of digital miscommunication requires a heightened awareness of the limitations of online dialogue. How do individuals decipher the unspoken nuances in digital messages? What strategies can couples employ to mitigate the risks of misunderstandings in the digital realm? As we explore the intricacies of digital communication, we unravel the ways in which couples navigate the potential pitfalls while harnessing the benefits of constant connection.

The Paradox of Distance and Closeness: Virtual connections, while enabling constant communication, introduce a paradox of distance and closeness in modern relationships. The digital realm, with its immediacy and accessibility, can simultaneously create a sense of distance as individuals navigate the challenges of maintaining authentic connection through screens. The paradox extends to long-distance relationships, where technology becomes both a lifeline and a reminder of physical separation.

In examining the paradox of distance and closeness, we delve into the emotional complexities of modern relationships. How do couples balance the benefits of constant connection with the challenges of maintaining genuine intimacy? How does technology shape the dynamics of long-distance relationships, and how do individuals navigate the delicate balance between virtual and physical presence?

Privacy and Boundaries in the Digital Realm: The digital age blurs the boundaries between public and private spheres, as individuals share aspects of their lives on social media platforms and through digital communication. The challenge of maintaining privacy and boundaries in the digital realm becomes a pertinent aspect of modern romance. Couples must negotiate the level of transparency and disclosure that feels comfortable, considering the impact of digital visibility on relationship dynamics.

As we explore the theme of privacy and boundaries, we delve into the ways in which technology challenges traditional notions of personal space. How do individuals navigate the balance between sharing and preserving their private lives in the digital age? What strategies can couples employ to establish healthy boundaries and ensure a sense of autonomy while participating in the interconnected landscape of online communication?

Technology as a Catalyst for Connection: Amidst the challenges and complexities, technology stands as a catalyst for connection, providing couples with tools to express affection, share experiences, and sustain meaningful relationships. The digital landscape becomes a canvas for modern romance, offering opportunities for creativity and innovation in how couples navigate the intricacies of communication and connection.

The role of technology as a catalyst for connection extends beyond the virtual realm to include shared digital experiences. Couples can engage in online activities, play digital games, or even create joint digital spaces, fostering a sense of togetherness despite physical separation. As we explore the ways in which technology acts as a facilitator for modern romance, we uncover the potential for creativity and collaboration in the digital space.

In unraveling the intricate layers of online communication and virtual connections, it becomes clear that technology has become an integral player in shaping the language of modern love. From the evolution of digital dialogue to the challenges of virtual intimacy, the digital landscape introduces both opportunities for connection and complexities to navigate. Join us as we continue our exploration of technological influences on modern romance, delving into the multifaceted ways in which online communication shapes the narrative of contemporary love.

Social Media's Impact on Relationship Dynamics

In the intricate tapestry of modern romance, the influence of technology extends beyond initial connections and digital communication to the very fabric of relationship dynamics. As we navigate the transformative landscape of contemporary love, this chapter delves into the profound impact of social media on how individuals perceive, express, and navigate their relationships in the digital age.

Constructing Digital Narratives: Social media platforms have become integral stages for individuals to construct and curate digital narratives of their relationships. Couples share moments of joy, milestones, and expressions of love through curated posts, photos, and stories, creating a digital storyline that reflects their idealized version of love. The act of sharing on social media becomes a means of public affirmation, reinforcing the connection between individuals and showcasing their relationship to a broader audience.

The construction of digital narratives raises questions about authenticity and the blurred lines between public and private spheres. How accurately do social media portrayals reflect the complexities of a relationship? What impact does the curated nature of digital narratives have on individuals' perceptions of their own relationships and those of others? As we explore social media's role in constructing digital narratives, we unravel the ways in which individuals navigate the tension between authenticity and the desire for external validation.

The Pressure of Perfection: Social media, with its curated imagery and filtered depictions of love, introduces a pressure for perfection in relationship dynamics. Couples may feel compelled to present an idealized version of their relationship to conform to societal expectations and the perceived norms set by influencers and celebrities. The pursuit of perfection, fueled by the desire for likes and comments, can create a gap between digital representations and the nuanced reality of relationships.

This pressure prompts a reflection on the impact of societal expectations on relationship dynamics. How does the pursuit of perfection on social media influence individuals' self-esteem and the dynamics of their relationships? How do couples navigate the delicate balance between presenting a positive image and embracing the authenticity of the highs and lows inherent in any partnership? As we explore the pressure of perfection, we dissect the ways in which social media shapes the emotional landscape of modern relationships.

External Validation and Relationship Satisfaction: The digital realm introduces a unique dynamic where external validation, in the form of likes, comments, and shares, becomes intertwined with individuals' perceptions of relationship satisfaction. Social media interactions act as a form of social proof, reinforcing the significance of digital affirmation in the contemporary narrative of love. The number of likes on a couple's photo or the engagement with their digital narratives can influence how individuals perceive the strength and validity of their relationships.

This reliance on external validation prompts an exploration of the emotional impact on individuals and couples. How does the quest for likes and social approval impact relationship satisfaction? What role does digital affirmation play in shaping individuals' self-esteem within the context of their romantic partnerships? As we delve into the interplay between external validation and relationship dynamics, we unravel the complexities of navigating love in the age of social media.

The Paradox of Connection and Disconnection: While social media offers a platform for connection, it introduces a paradoxical dynamic where individuals may feel simultaneously connected and disconnected from their partners. The constant stream of digital stimuli, notifications, and updates can create a sense of perpetual connection, yet this digital tethering may not necessarily translate into genuine emotional intimacy.

This paradox prompts reflection on the quality of connection fostered by social media. How does the constant flow of digital information impact individuals' ability to be present and engaged in their relationships? How do couples navigate the delicate balance between staying connected in the digital realm and fostering authentic emotional closeness? As we explore the paradox of connection and disconnection, we unravel the ways in which social media influences the texture of modern relationship dynamics.

Navigating Digital Jealousy and Comparison: The curated nature of social media can give rise to digital jealousy and comparison within relationships. Individuals may find themselves comparing their partnerships to the seemingly perfect relationships depicted on their social media feeds, leading to feelings of inadequacy or discontent. The digital landscape becomes a breeding ground for comparison, as couples measure their own relationship milestones against the idealized portrayals of others.

The exploration of digital jealousy and comparison delves into the emotional impact on individuals and couples. How do these dynamics influence self-esteem and satisfaction within relationships? What strategies can individuals employ to navigate the challenges of comparison in the digital age? As we unravel the complexities of navigating jealousy and comparison on social media, we explore the ways in which couples redefine their understanding of success and fulfillment in modern romance.

Social Media's Role in Relationship Conflict: The interconnected nature of social media introduces a new dimension to relationship conflict, as disagreements and misunderstandings may play out in the public arena. Couples may find themselves navigating conflicts not only in private but also under the scrutiny of their digital audience. The potential for public airing of grievances raises questions about the impact of social media on the dynamics of conflict resolution within romantic partnerships.

This examination of social media's role in relationship conflict explores the challenges couples face when addressing disagreements in the public eye. How does the digital landscape impact the resolution of conflicts, and what strategies can couples employ to maintain a sense of privacy and dignity? As we navigate the intricacies of relationship conflict on social media, we uncover the ways in which technology reshapes the terrain of disagreement and resolution.

Unveiling the Impact on Mental Health: The pervasive presence of social media in modern relationships also raises concerns about its impact on mental health. The constant exposure to curated narratives, external validation, and comparison dynamics can contribute to heightened stress, anxiety, and feelings of inadequacy. The pressure to maintain a positive online image may lead to emotional strain and exhaustion, impacting individuals' mental well-being within the context of their romantic partnerships.

This exploration of social media's impact on mental health delves into the nuanced relationship between digital engagement and emotional well-being. How does the pursuit of a curated online presence impact individuals' mental health within the context of their romantic relationships? What strategies can individuals employ to foster a healthy balance between digital engagement and mental well-being? As we navigate the intricate terrain of mental health in the digital age, we uncover the ways in which social media influences the emotional landscape of modern love.

Strategies for Navigating Social Media in Relationships: In the face of the complexities introduced by social media, individuals and couples must navigate this digital terrain with intentionality and mindfulness. Strategies for managing social media in relationships involve establishing healthy boundaries, fostering open communication, and consciously curating a digital presence that aligns with authentic values. Couples can engage in honest conversations about their digital preferences, comfort levels, and expectations, creating a shared understanding of how social media fits into their relationship dynamics.

This exploration of strategies for navigating social media in relationships uncovers the ways in which individuals and couples can harness the benefits of digital engagement while mitigating potential pitfalls. How can couples create a digital environment that supports their relationship goals? What role does open communication play in fostering a healthy approach to social media within partnerships? As we delve into the realm of strategies for navigating social media, we uncover the pathways to fostering meaningful connections in the age of digital interconnectedness.

In unraveling the profound impact of social media on relationship dynamics, it becomes clear that the digital landscape introduces both opportunities for connection and challenges to navigate. From the construction of digital narratives to the pressures of perfection and external validation, social media shapes the narrative of modern love. Join us as we continue our exploration of technological influences on modern romance, delving into the multifaceted ways in which social media influences the dynamics of contemporary relationships.

Tech Innovations Redefining Modern Dating

In the ever-evolving landscape of modern romance, technological innovations continue to redefine the very essence of dating. As we navigate the transformative journey of contemporary love, this chapter explores the profound impact of tech innovations on the intricate dance of modern dating. From virtual matchmaking algorithms to innovative ways of connecting, technology emerges as a dynamic force reshaping the very fabric of romantic courtship.

Algorithms and the Art of Matchmaking: One of the most revolutionary advancements in modern dating is the integration of sophisticated algorithms into matchmaking platforms. Dating apps employ complex algorithms that analyze user preferences, behavior, and demographic data to curate potential matches. This data-driven approach aims to enhance compatibility, presenting users with a curated selection of individuals who align with their interests and values.

The algorithmic approach to matchmaking raises intriguing questions about the role of data in the quest for love. How do these algorithms navigate the delicate balance between scientific analysis and the serendipity of genuine connection? What impact does the algorithmic approach have on individuals' perceptions of choice and compatibility in the realm of modern dating? As we explore the world of matchmaking algorithms, we unravel the ways in which technology shapes the initial stages of connection in contemporary romance.

The Rise of Niche Dating Platforms: Tech innovations in dating extend beyond generic matchmaking to the rise of niche dating platforms catering to specific interests, lifestyles, and communities. From platforms dedicated to specific professions to those focusing on shared hobbies or cultural affinities, niche dating apps offer individuals the opportunity to connect with like-minded partners who share a deeper resonance beyond traditional factors.

The proliferation of niche dating platforms prompts reflection on the significance of shared interests in modern relationships. How do these specialized platforms impact the dynamics of connection and compatibility? What role do niche dating apps play in fostering a sense of community within the dating landscape? As we delve into the world of niche dating, we uncover the ways in which technology allows individuals to navigate the vast tapestry of contemporary romance with greater specificity.

Virtual Dating and the Age of Connectivity: The advent of virtual reality (VR) and augmented reality (AR) technologies has ushered in a new era of dating experiences. Virtual dating platforms enable individuals to connect in immersive digital environments, transcending physical distances and providing a unique avenue for shared experiences. From virtual reality date nights to augmented reality adventures, technology redefines the boundaries of traditional dating, offering couples novel ways to engage and connect.

The exploration of virtual dating prompts consideration of the role of technology in fostering emotional closeness. How do virtual experiences contribute to the depth of connection between individuals? What impact does the digitization of dating have on the traditional notions of physical presence and shared space? As we navigate the realm of virtual dating, we unravel the ways in which technology expands the possibilities of romantic connection in the digital age.

The Intersection of AI and Personalized Dating Experiences: Artificial Intelligence (AI) plays a pivotal role in shaping personalized dating experiences, offering individuals tailored recommendations and insights based on their preferences and behaviors. AI-driven dating apps can analyze patterns in user data to provide personalized suggestions, from ideal date locations to conversation starters. This level of personalization aims to enhance the user experience and streamline the dating process.

The integration of AI in dating introduces considerations about privacy and ethical use of personal data. How do individuals navigate the balance between personalized recommendations and concerns about data security? What role does transparency play in fostering trust between users and dating platforms? As we explore the intersection of AI and personalized dating experiences, we unravel the ways in which technology transforms the landscape of individualized romantic connections.

Live Streaming and Real-Time Connections: Live streaming technologies have emerged as a dynamic tool in modern dating, allowing individuals to connect in real-time and share authentic moments. Dating apps incorporating live streaming features enable users to engage in virtual interactions, fostering a sense of immediacy and spontaneity. From live video chats to virtual events, technology facilitates real-time connections that transcend the limitations of traditional text-based communication.

The exploration of live streaming in dating prompts reflection on the impact of authentic, unfiltered interactions. How do real-time connections contribute to the development of genuine intimacy? What challenges and opportunities arise when individuals share unscripted moments through live streaming? As we delve into the world of real-time connections, we uncover the ways in which technology redefines the dynamics of spontaneity and authenticity in modern dating.

Blockchain and the Future of Trust in Dating: Blockchain technology has begun to permeate the dating landscape, offering solutions to challenges related to trust, authenticity, and security. Decentralized platforms built on blockchain principles aim to provide users with greater control over their data, enhance transparency in user interactions, and mitigate issues such as catfishing and fraudulent profiles. The integration of blockchain introduces a new paradigm in which trust becomes a foundational element of digital dating.

The examination of blockchain in dating raises questions about the future of trust and security in online interactions. How does decentralized technology contribute to creating a safer and more trustworthy dating environment? What implications does blockchain have for the balance between transparency and privacy in the digital dating landscape? As we explore the role of blockchain in dating, we unravel the ways in which technology evolves to address challenges and enhance the integrity of online connections.

Biometric Data and Emotional Compatibility: Advancements in biometric technology offer a glimpse into a future where dating platforms may leverage physiological data to enhance the understanding of emotional compatibility. Wearable devices and biometric sensors can track users' physiological responses during interactions, providing insights into emotional states and compatibility markers. The integration of biometric data introduces a layer of scientific analysis to the assessment of emotional connection in modern dating.

The exploration of biometric data in dating prompts consideration of ethical considerations and user consent. How do individuals navigate the balance between enhanced compatibility insights and concerns about privacy? What role does transparency play in fostering user trust when it comes to the collection and use of biometric information? As we delve into the potential of biometric data in dating, we unravel the ways in which technology pushes the boundaries of understanding emotional dynamics in romantic connections.

In navigating the landscape of tech innovations redefining modern dating, it becomes evident that technology is not merely a tool but a dynamic force shaping the very essence of contemporary romance. From algorithms guiding initial matches to the immersive experiences of virtual dating, innovation paves the way for novel approaches to connection. Join us as we continue our exploration of technological influences on modern romance, delving into the multifaceted ways in which tech innovations transform the art of courtship in the 21st century.

Chapter 2: Changing Dynamics of Romantic Relationships

Evolving Notions of Love and Commitment

In the kaleidoscope of modern romance, the very notions of love and commitment are undergoing a profound transformation. As we navigate the complex terrain of changing dynamics in romantic relationships, this chapter delves into the evolving nature of love and commitment in the 21st century. From shifting paradigms to redefined expectations, the exploration unfolds the intricacies of how contemporary relationships are reshaping the foundations of emotional connection.

From Tradition to Fluidity: Traditional notions of love and commitment were often characterized by clear societal expectations and predefined milestones. However, the 21st century has witnessed a departure from these rigid structures, giving rise to a more fluid and personalized approach to romantic relationships. The evolution from tradition to fluidity allows individuals the freedom to define the terms of their own relationships, moving away from predetermined scripts towards narratives crafted based on personal preferences and authentic connection.

This shift prompts reflection on the role of societal expectations in shaping individuals' understanding of love and commitment. How do evolving notions of fluidity impact the way couples navigate their relationships? What challenges and opportunities arise when individuals have the agency to redefine the parameters of love according to their unique needs and desires? As we explore the journey from tradition to fluidity, we unravel the ways in which modern relationships redefine the very essence of love.

The Spectrum of Relationship Styles: Contemporary romantic relationships showcase a spectrum of styles, ranging from traditional monogamy to various forms of non-traditional partnerships. The recognition and acceptance of diverse relationship styles, including polyamory, open relationships, and ethical non-monogamy, challenge the monolithic understanding of love and commitment. This broad spectrum allows individuals to choose relationship structures that align with their values, fostering a sense of autonomy in the pursuit of meaningful connections.

The exploration of the spectrum of relationship styles raises questions about societal acceptance and understanding. How do individuals navigate the complexities of diverse relationship styles in the face of societal norms? What role does open communication play in establishing mutual understanding and consent within non-traditional partnerships? As we delve into the spectrum of relationship styles, we uncover the ways in which modern relationships redefine the landscape of commitment.

Dynamic Interplay of Independence and Partnership: Evolving notions of love and commitment in the 21st century highlight the dynamic interplay between individual independence and the desire for partnership. Modern relationships acknowledge and celebrate the importance of personal growth and autonomy within the context of a romantic partnership. The traditional dichotomy of independence versus partnership transforms into a more nuanced understanding that values both individual fulfillment and shared connection.

The examination of the dynamic interplay prompts reflection on the balance between independence and partnership. How do individuals navigate the tension between personal aspirations and shared goals within the context of a romantic relationship? What role does mutual support play in fostering a dynamic interplay that nurtures both individual and collective growth? As we explore the dynamic interplay of independence and partnership, we unravel the ways in which modern relationships redefine the boundaries of commitment.

The Evolution of Emotional Intimacy: Emotional intimacy, a cornerstone of romantic relationships, undergoes a nuanced evolution in the contemporary landscape. The traditional pathways to emotional connection are augmented by digital communication, allowing couples to navigate the complexities of intimacy beyond physical proximity. The digital age introduces new avenues for emotional expression, from heartfelt messages to real-time video calls, reshaping the dynamics of how individuals connect on an emotional level.

The exploration of the evolution of emotional intimacy delves into the impact of technology on the depth and quality of connections. How do digital interactions contribute to emotional closeness, and what challenges arise in the absence of traditional face-to-face intimacy? How do individuals navigate the balance between virtual expressions of love and the need for physical closeness? As we unravel the evolution of emotional intimacy, we uncover the ways in which modern relationships redefine the parameters of emotional connection.

Reimagining Commitment Beyond Conventions: The 21st century witnesses a reimagining of commitment that extends beyond conventional markers such as marriage or long-term cohabitation. Couples increasingly define commitment based on shared values, mutual respect, and ongoing communication rather than adherence to societal norms. The reimagining of commitment allows individuals to craft partnerships that align with their personal journeys, fostering a sense of dedication that transcends traditional boundaries.

This reimagining prompts reflection on the role of societal expectations in defining commitment. How do couples navigate the pressure to conform to conventional markers of commitment, and what alternative narratives emerge when commitment is redefined? What role does ongoing communication play in establishing a shared understanding of commitment within a relationship? As we explore the reimagining of commitment, we unravel the ways in which modern relationships redefine the essence of dedication and loyalty.

Intersection of Individualism and Partnership: The paradigm of individualism shapes the landscape of modern romantic relationships, with individuals placing a premium on personal growth, self-discovery, and fulfillment. This emphasis on individualism intersects with the desire for partnership, creating a unique dynamic where couples navigate the tension between self-expression and shared connection. The intersection of individualism and partnership prompts a reevaluation of the traditional narratives surrounding sacrifice and compromise in relationships.

The exploration of the intersection raises questions about the compatibility of individual aspirations within the context of partnership. How do couples negotiate the balance between personal ambitions and shared goals? What strategies can individuals employ to support each other's individual journeys while fostering a sense of unity in their partnership? As we delve into the intersection of individualism and partnership, we uncover the ways in which modern relationships redefine the boundaries of commitment.

Fluidity in Relationship Milestones: The evolution of love and commitment in the 21st century is accompanied by a fluidity in the recognition of relationship milestones. Traditional markers such as marriage and parenthood no longer serve as universal benchmarks, allowing couples to define their own significant moments. The fluidity in milestones embraces a diversity of paths, acknowledging that each relationship follows a unique trajectory shaped by the values and aspirations of the individuals involved.

The examination of fluidity in relationship milestones prompts reflection on the role of societal expectations in shaping individuals' life trajectories. How do couples navigate the pressure to adhere to conventional milestones, and what alternative narratives emerge when milestones are redefined? What role does mutual understanding and communication play in establishing shared goals and significant moments within a relationship? As we explore the fluidity in relationship milestones, we unravel the ways in which modern relationships redefine the journey of commitment.

Challenges and Opportunities in Evolving Notions: The evolving notions of love and commitment in modern relationships bring forth both challenges and opportunities. While the freedom to redefine the parameters of commitment allows for greater individual expression, it also requires ongoing communication and negotiation between partners. The challenges may include navigating societal expectations, managing differing expectations within the partnership, and establishing a shared understanding of commitment.

The exploration of challenges and opportunities prompts reflection on the resilience and adaptability required in modern relationships. How do couples overcome challenges related to evolving notions of love and commitment, and what strategies contribute to the success of these partnerships? How can individuals and couples seize the opportunities presented by the freedom to redefine their relationship dynamics? As we delve into the complexities of evolving notions, we uncover the ways in which modern relationships navigate the terrain of commitment with resilience and intentionality.

In unraveling the evolving notions of love and commitment, it becomes clear that modern relationships are dynamic, multifaceted, and deeply personal. From fluidity in milestones to the intersection of individualism and partnership, the evolving landscape of romantic connections reflects the diverse and unique journeys individuals embark upon. Join us as we continue our exploration of changing dynamics in romantic relationships, delving into the shifting paradigms that shape the very essence of love in the 21st century.

Shifting Gender Roles in Modern Relationships

In the intricate tapestry of modern romance, the threads of gender roles are undergoing a profound reweaving. As we navigate the evolving landscape of romantic relationships, this chapter delves into the shifting dynamics of gender roles in the 21st century. From traditional expectations to the pursuit of equality, the exploration unfolds the complexities of how contemporary relationships redefine the roles individuals play in the pursuit of love and connection.

From Prescribed Roles to Fluid Identities: Historically, romantic relationships were often framed within prescribed gender roles, assigning specific expectations and responsibilities based on societal norms. However, the 21st century marks a departure from these rigid structures, embracing a more fluid and dynamic understanding of gender identities within relationships. The journey from prescribed roles to fluid identities allows individuals to explore and express their authentic selves, unbound by traditional expectations.

The exploration of fluid identities prompts reflection on the impact of societal expectations on individual expression within relationships. How do shifting gender roles contribute to the authenticity and self-discovery of individuals in romantic partnerships? What challenges and opportunities arise when couples navigate the complexities of breaking away from prescribed roles? As we delve into the transition from prescribed roles to fluid identities, we unravel the ways in which modern relationships redefine the expression of gender within the context of love.

Balancing Autonomy and Interdependence: The shift in gender dynamics within modern relationships is marked by a pursuit of balance between autonomy and interdependence. Couples increasingly embrace the principles of equality, valuing each partner's autonomy while fostering a sense of interdependence in shared decision-making and responsibilities. The traditional dichotomy of dominant and submissive roles transforms into a more egalitarian approach that honors the agency of both individuals within the partnership.

The exploration of balancing autonomy and interdependence prompts reflection on the negotiation of power dynamics within relationships. How do couples navigate the delicate balance between individual autonomy and shared responsibilities? What role does effective communication play in establishing a sense of equality within the partnership? As we delve into the pursuit of balance, we uncover the ways in which modern relationships redefine the power dynamics inherent in gender roles.

Reimagining Provider and Caregiver Roles: Traditional gender roles often assigned specific provider and caregiver roles based on gender, perpetuating stereotypes that linked masculinity with financial provision and femininity with nurturing responsibilities. However, the evolving dynamics of modern relationships challenge these stereotypes, reimagining provider and caregiver roles based on individual strengths, preferences, and aspirations. Couples are increasingly embracing flexibility in how they distribute responsibilities related to both financial provision and caregiving.

The reimagining of provider and caregiver roles prompts reflection on the impact of stereotypes on the division of labor within relationships. How do couples navigate the negotiation of responsibilities in a way that honors individual strengths and preferences? What challenges and opportunities arise when individuals are freed from the constraints of traditional provider and caregiver roles? As we explore the reimagining of roles, we unravel the ways in which modern relationships redefine the distribution of responsibilities based on merit rather than gender.

Equal Partnership in Decision-Making: The quest for equality within modern relationships extends to decision-making processes, challenging the traditional model where certain decisions were often relegated to one partner based on gender. In contemporary romance, the principle of equal partnership emphasizes shared decision-making, where both individuals actively contribute to choices that impact their lives. The traditional notion of one partner holding more decision-making power gives way to collaborative processes that value the input of both individuals.

The exploration of equal partnership in decision-making prompts reflection on the importance of communication and respect within relationships. How do couples establish a foundation of mutual decision-making that reflects the principles of equality? What role does open communication play in navigating disagreements and differences of opinion within the context of shared decision-making? As we delve into the concept of equal partnership, we uncover the ways in which modern relationships redefine the dynamics of decision-making based on collaboration and respect.

Redefined Expectations in Emotional Expression: The shifting dynamics of gender roles in modern relationships extend to the realm of emotional expression, challenging traditional expectations that linked masculinity with emotional restraint and femininity with nurturing emotions.

Contemporary relationships encourage individuals to express their emotions authentically, breaking away from the constraints of gender norms that may have hindered open communication in the past. Emotional vulnerability becomes a valued aspect of modern relationships, fostering deeper connections between partners.

The exploration of redefined expectations in emotional expression prompts reflection on the impact of societal norms on individuals' ability to communicate authentically within relationships. How do couples navigate the challenges associated with breaking away from traditional expectations in emotional expression? What role does emotional intelligence play in fostering a supportive and communicative environment within the partnership? As we delve into redefined expectations, we uncover the ways in which modern relationships reshape the landscape of emotional expression based on authenticity and vulnerability.

Shared Parenting and Co-Responsibility: The evolution of gender roles within modern relationships is particularly pronounced in the realm of parenting and co-responsibility. Traditional expectations often placed the primary burden of childcare on women, reinforcing gendered stereotypes related to nurturing and caregiving. However, contemporary relationships witness a departure from these norms, with couples increasingly embracing shared parenting and co-responsibility for both domestic and childcare duties.

The exploration of shared parenting and co-responsibility prompts reflection on the impact of evolving gender roles on family dynamics. How do couples negotiate the distribution of domestic and parenting responsibilities in a way that reflects equality? What challenges and opportunities arise when both partners actively contribute to the caregiving aspect of their family? As we delve into shared parenting and co-responsibility, we unravel the ways in which modern relationships redefine the concept of partnership within the context of family life.

Navigating External Perceptions and Pressures: While couples may embrace evolving gender roles within their relationships, external perceptions and societal pressures can pose challenges. Judgment and scrutiny from others may influence how couples navigate their roles, potentially creating tensions or misunderstandings. Navigating external perceptions and pressures requires a level of resilience and conviction to uphold the principles of equality and authenticity within the partnership.

The exploration of external perceptions and pressures prompts reflection on the importance of communication and solidarity within relationships. How do couples support each other in the face of external judgments related to their roles within the partnership? What strategies can individuals employ to maintain a sense of autonomy and authenticity despite societal expectations? As we delve into navigating external perceptions and pressures, we uncover the ways in which modern relationships fortify themselves against external influences to maintain a foundation of equality and authenticity.

Educational and Professional Pursuits: The shifting dynamics of gender roles in modern relationships extend to educational and professional pursuits, challenging traditional expectations related to career choices and ambitions. Contemporary couples recognize the importance of supporting each other's educational and career goals, fostering an environment where individuals can pursue their passions and aspirations regardless of gender. The traditional limitations imposed by gendered expectations in educational and professional pursuits give way to a more supportive and egalitarian approach.

The exploration of educational and professional pursuits prompts reflection on the impact of evolving gender roles on individual fulfillment and career satisfaction. How do couples navigate the complexities of balancing career ambitions with personal and family life? What role does mutual support play in creating an environment that fosters the pursuit of educational and professional goals without gender-based restrictions? As we delve into the realm of educational and professional pursuits, we uncover the ways in which modern relationships redefine the landscape of career aspirations based on merit rather than gender.

Challenges and Opportunities in Shifting Dynamics: The shifting dynamics of gender roles within modern relationships bring forth both challenges and opportunities. While the pursuit of equality and authenticity offers couples the freedom to redefine their roles, it also requires ongoing communication and negotiation. The challenges may include navigating external pressures, managing differing expectations within the partnership, and establishing a shared understanding of evolving gender dynamics.

The exploration of challenges and opportunities prompts reflection on the adaptability and resilience required in modern relationships. How do couples overcome challenges related to shifting gender roles, and what strategies contribute to the success of these partnerships? How can individuals and couples seize the opportunities presented by the freedom to redefine their roles based on mutual respect and equality? As we delve into the complexities of shifting dynamics, we uncover the ways in which modern relationships navigate the terrain of evolving gender roles with resilience and intentionality.

In unraveling the shifting dynamics of gender roles, it becomes evident that modern relationships are characterized by flexibility, equality, and a commitment to authenticity. From fluid identities to shared responsibilities, the evolving landscape of romantic connections reflects the diverse and unique journeys individuals embark upon. Join us as we continue our exploration of changing dynamics in romantic relationships, delving into the shifting paradigms that shape the very essence of love in the 21st century.

Impact of Individualism on Partnership

In the intricate dance of modern romance, the dynamics of partnership are undergoing a profound transformation shaped by the currents of individualism. As we navigate the evolving landscape of romantic relationships, this chapter delves into the impact of individualism on the very fabric of partnership in the 21st century. From the celebration of personal autonomy to the challenges of maintaining connection, the exploration unfolds the complexities of how contemporary relationships navigate the intersection of individual desires and shared connections.

Celebrating Personal Autonomy: One of the defining features of the 21st-century romantic landscape is the celebration of personal autonomy within partnerships. Individuals, influenced by the principles of individualism, seek to maintain a sense of independence and self-fulfillment even within the context of a romantic relationship. The celebration of personal autonomy prompts couples to appreciate and support each other's individual pursuits, fostering an environment where both partners can thrive independently.

This celebration prompts reflection on the balance between personal autonomy and shared connection within modern relationships. How do couples navigate the tension between individual aspirations and the desire for partnership? What strategies contribute to the cultivation of a supportive environment that allows each partner to pursue personal growth and fulfillment? As we explore the celebration of personal autonomy, we unravel the ways in which modern relationships redefine the boundaries between independence and connection.

Navigating the Pursuit of Personal Goals: Individualism shapes the pursuit of personal goals within modern partnerships, emphasizing the importance of supporting each other's individual aspirations. Couples, influenced by the principles of individualism, actively navigate the complexities of balancing personal ambitions with shared responsibilities. The traditional dichotomy that may have limited personal pursuits for the sake of the relationship gives way to a more fluid and collaborative approach that honors both individual and shared goals.

The exploration of the pursuit of personal goals prompts reflection on the negotiation of priorities within modern relationships. How do couples support each other in the pursuit of individual goals without sacrificing the health of the partnership? What role does effective communication play in establishing a shared understanding of each other's aspirations? As we delve into the pursuit of personal goals, we uncover the ways in which modern relationships navigate the delicate balance between individual aspirations and shared commitments.

Embracing Diversity in Interests and Hobbies: The influence of individualism on modern partnerships extends to the realm of interests and hobbies, fostering an environment where couples embrace the diversity of each other's passions. Unlike traditional models that may have emphasized shared interests, contemporary relationships celebrate the uniqueness of individual hobbies, recognizing that each partner contributes to the relationship with their own set of interests and pursuits.

The exploration of diversity in interests and hobbies prompts reflection on the role of individual passions in enhancing the overall quality of the partnership. How do couples navigate the complexities of differing interests while maintaining a sense of connection? What strategies contribute to the creation of a supportive environment that allows each partner to pursue their hobbies without feeling constrained by traditional expectations? As we delve into the embrace of diversity, we unravel the ways in which modern relationships redefine the concept of shared interests within the context of individualism.

Balancing Me Time and We Time: Individualism introduces a nuanced approach to the balance between personal time (Me Time) and shared time as a couple (We Time). Unlike traditional models that may have emphasized constant togetherness, modern relationships recognize the importance of carving out space for individual pursuits and self-reflection. The pursuit of personal fulfillment through Me Time becomes an integral aspect of the partnership, contributing to the overall health and resilience of the relationship.

The exploration of balancing Me Time and We Time prompts reflection on the negotiation of boundaries within modern relationships. How do couples establish a balance that allows for personal growth and self-care without neglecting the shared aspects of their relationship? What role does open communication play in navigating the complexities of individual and shared time? As we delve into the balance between Me Time and We Time, we uncover the ways in which modern relationships redefine the concept of togetherness within the context of individualism.

Shifting Dynamics of Decision-Making: The impact of individualism on partnership is particularly pronounced in the shifting dynamics of decision-making within modern relationships. Unlike traditional models that may have relied on hierarchical structures, contemporary couples emphasize egalitarian approaches to decision-making. The principles of individualism contribute to a more collaborative process, where both partners actively contribute to choices that impact their lives.

The exploration of shifting dynamics in decision-making prompts reflection on the negotiation of power within modern relationships. How do couples establish a foundation of mutual decision-making that reflects the principles of equality and individual agency? What role does open communication play in navigating disagreements and differences of opinion within the context of shared decision-making? As we delve into shifting dynamics, we uncover the ways in which modern relationships redefine the power structures inherent in partnership within the context of individualism.

Navigating Personal Growth and Change: Individualism introduces a profound shift in the approach to personal growth and change within modern partnerships. Unlike traditional models that may have expected individuals to conform to static roles, contemporary relationships actively support and navigate the personal evolution of each partner. The celebration of personal growth becomes a shared value, fostering an environment where individuals feel encouraged to explore new facets of themselves without fear of jeopardizing the relationship.

The exploration of personal growth and change prompts reflection on the role of adaptability and support within modern relationships. How do couples navigate the challenges and opportunities associated with personal evolution? What strategies contribute to the creation of a supportive environment that allows for individual growth without compromising the stability of the partnership? As we delve into personal growth and change, we uncover the ways in which modern relationships redefine the concept of stability within the context of individualism.

The Impact of Technology on Individual Expression: The digital age amplifies the influence of individualism within modern relationships, particularly through the impact of technology on individual expression. Social media platforms, blogs, and other online spaces provide individuals with avenues for self-expression, allowing them to share their thoughts, experiences, and personal narratives with a broader audience. The digital realm becomes an extension of individual identity, influencing how individuals present themselves within the context of their romantic partnerships.

The exploration of the impact of technology prompts reflection on the role of online spaces in shaping individual expression and identity. How do couples navigate the complexities of online self-presentation and its impact on the relationship? What challenges and opportunities arise when technology becomes a tool for individual expression within the context of partnership? As we delve into the impact of technology, we uncover the ways in which modern relationships redefine the boundaries between online and offline identities within the context of individualism.

Challenges and Opportunities in Individualism: The impact of individualism on partnership brings forth both challenges and opportunities. While the celebration of personal autonomy and individual growth contributes to the richness of modern relationships, it also requires ongoing communication and negotiation. The challenges may include navigating differences in priorities, managing Me Time and We Time, and establishing a shared understanding of evolving dynamics.

The exploration of challenges and opportunities prompts reflection on the resilience and adaptability required in modern relationships. How do couples overcome challenges related to individualism, and what strategies contribute to the success of these partnerships? How can individuals and couples seize the opportunities presented by the celebration of personal autonomy and the pursuit of individual goals within the context of partnership? As we delve into the complexities of individualism, we uncover the ways in which modern relationships navigate the terrain of evolving dynamics with resilience and intentionality.

In unraveling the impact of individualism on partnership, it becomes evident that modern relationships are characterized by flexibility, equality, and a commitment to authenticity. From celebrating personal autonomy to navigating the dynamics of decision-making, the evolving landscape of romantic connections reflects the diverse and unique journeys individuals embark upon. Join us as we continue our exploration of changing dynamics in romantic relationships, delving into the shifting paradigms that shape the very essence of love in the 21st century.

Diversity in Relationship Structures Today

In the kaleidoscope of modern romance, the contours of relationship structures are undergoing a profound transformation, embracing a rich diversity that challenges traditional norms. As we navigate the evolving landscape of romantic relationships, this chapter delves into the myriad ways in which diversity in relationship structures defines the 21st-century love story. From polyamory to unconventional partnerships, the exploration unfolds the complexities of how contemporary relationships navigate and celebrate diverse structures that defy conventional expectations.

Embracing Non-Traditional Paths: The 21st century witnesses a departure from conventional relationship structures, with individuals and couples embracing non-traditional paths that deviate from the monolithic model of monogamous, long-term partnerships. The spectrum of non-traditional relationship structures includes various forms of polyamory, open relationships, ethical non-monogamy, and other arrangements that prioritize transparency, consent, and the recognition of diverse expressions of love.

The exploration of non-traditional paths prompts reflection on the motivations and values that drive individuals to embrace alternative relationship structures. How do couples navigate the complexities of unconventional partnerships while maintaining open communication and mutual consent? What role does societal acceptance play in shaping individuals' decisions to explore non-traditional paths, and how do they challenge traditional norms? As we delve into embracing non-traditional paths, we uncover the ways in which modern relationships redefine the landscape of commitment and connection.

Polyamory and the Evolution of Commitment: Polyamory, characterized by consensual and ethical relationships with multiple partners, stands as a prominent feature in the tapestry of diverse relationship structures. The evolution of commitment within polyamorous relationships challenges traditional notions of exclusivity, introducing a dynamic where individuals can form meaningful connections with multiple partners simultaneously. The exploration of polyamory prompts reflection on the foundations of commitment and the negotiation of boundaries within these complex relationship dynamics.

How do individuals in polyamorous relationships navigate the intricacies of commitment and emotional connection with multiple partners? What challenges and opportunities arise in balancing the needs and desires of multiple individuals within a polyamorous dynamic? What role does open communication play in establishing trust and understanding among partners in polyamorous relationships? As we delve into polyamory and the evolution of commitment, we uncover the ways in which modern relationships redefine the traditional parameters of exclusivity and loyalty.

Open Relationships and Communication Dynamics: Open relationships, characterized by consensually engaging in romantic or sexual interactions with individuals outside the primary partnership, offer a distinct perspective on communication dynamics within contemporary relationships. The exploration of open relationships prompts reflection on the role of communication in establishing clear boundaries, managing expectations, and fostering trust among partners. How do individuals in open relationships navigate the delicate balance between freedom and commitment? What strategies contribute to effective communication and conflict resolution within the context of open relationships?

The exploration of open relationships prompts reflection on the role of communication in establishing clear boundaries, managing expectations, and fostering trust among partners. How do individuals in open relationships navigate the delicate balance between freedom and commitment? What strategies contribute to effective communication and conflict resolution within the context of open relationships? As we delve into open relationships and communication dynamics, we uncover the ways in which modern relationships redefine the boundaries of commitment and autonomy.

Ethical Non-Monogamy and Mutual Consent: Ethical non-monogamy, encompassing a range of consensually non-exclusive relationship structures, emphasizes the importance of mutual consent and transparency among all involved parties. The exploration of ethical non-monogamy prompts reflection on the role of consent as a cornerstone of modern relationships. How do individuals navigate the negotiation of boundaries and expectations within ethical non-monogamous dynamics? What challenges and opportunities arise in fostering a sense of trust and understanding among all parties involved?

As we delve into ethical non-monogamy and mutual consent, we uncover the ways in which modern relationships redefine the principles of trust, communication, and consent in the pursuit of diverse and consensual relationship structures.

Unconventional Partnerships and Unique Bonds: Beyond polyamory, open relationships, and ethical non-monogamy, modern relationships also embrace various unconventional partnerships and unique bonds. This may include asexual relationships, long-distance partnerships, or unions that challenge traditional expectations. The exploration of unconventional partnerships prompts reflection on the unique dynamics that define each relationship structure. How do individuals in unconventional partnerships navigate societal expectations and judgments? What strategies contribute to the strength and resilience of unique bonds that deviate from traditional norms?

The exploration of unconventional partnerships prompts reflection on the unique dynamics that define each relationship structure. How do individuals in unconventional partnerships navigate societal expectations and judgments? What strategies contribute to the strength and resilience of unique bonds that deviate from traditional norms? As we delve into unconventional partnerships and unique bonds, we uncover the ways in which modern relationships redefine the spectrum of connection and commitment.

Diverse Expressions of Love and Intimacy: Diversity in relationship structures also influences the expressions of love and intimacy within modern partnerships. The exploration of diverse expressions prompts reflection on the ways in which individuals and couples navigate the intricacies of love in its various forms. How do individuals in diverse relationship structures express and receive love? What challenges and opportunities arise in fostering intimacy within unconventional partnerships? What role does open communication play in establishing a shared understanding of love in its diverse manifestations?

The exploration of diverse expressions prompts reflection on the ways in which individuals and couples navigate the intricacies of love in its various forms. How do individuals in diverse relationship structures express and receive love? What challenges and opportunities arise in fostering intimacy within unconventional partnerships? What role does open communication play in establishing a shared understanding of love in its diverse manifestations? As we delve into diverse expressions of love and intimacy, we uncover the ways in which modern relationships redefine the language of connection and emotional fulfillment.

Intersectionality and Inclusivity: The impact of diversity in relationship structures extends beyond individual partnerships to embrace the principles of intersectionality and inclusivity. The exploration of intersectionality prompts reflection on how factors such as race, gender, sexual orientation, and socioeconomic status intersect with diverse relationship structures. How do individuals navigate the intersectionality of their identities within the context of non-traditional partnerships? What challenges and opportunities arise in fostering inclusivity and understanding among diverse communities?

The exploration of intersectionality prompts reflection on how factors such as race, gender, sexual orientation, and socioeconomic status intersect with diverse relationship structures. How do individuals navigate the intersectionality of their identities within the context of non-traditional partnerships? What challenges and opportunities arise in fostering inclusivity and understanding among diverse communities? As we delve into intersectionality and inclusivity, we uncover the ways in which modern relationships redefine the boundaries of acceptance and celebrate the richness of diverse narratives.

Challenges and Opportunities in Diverse Structures: The embrace of diversity in relationship structures brings forth both challenges and opportunities. While the celebration of non-traditional paths allows for greater individual expression and freedom, it also requires ongoing communication, negotiation, and societal acceptance. The challenges may include navigating external judgments, managing differing expectations within the partnership, and establishing a shared understanding of evolving dynamics.

The exploration of challenges and opportunities prompts reflection on the adaptability and resilience required in modern relationships. How do individuals and couples overcome challenges related to diverse relationship structures, and what strategies contribute to the success of these partnerships? How can societal attitudes shift to foster greater inclusivity and acceptance of diverse relationship structures? As we delve into the complexities of diverse structures, we uncover the ways in which modern relationships navigate the terrain of evolving dynamics with resilience and intentionality.

In unraveling the tapestry of diversity in relationship structures, it becomes evident that modern relationships are characterized by fluidity, acceptance, and a commitment to redefining the boundaries of connection. From polyamory to unconventional partnerships, the evolving landscape of romantic connections reflects the diverse and unique journeys individuals embark upon. Join us as we continue our exploration of changing dynamics in romantic relationships, delving into the shifting paradigms that shape the very essence of love in the 21st century.

Chapter 3: Celebrity Influence on Valentine's Day Trends

Pop Culture Icons Shaping Romantic Ideals

In the age of instant connectivity and pervasive media, the influence of pop culture icons on shaping romantic ideals has become a potent force in the realm of modern relationships. This chapter explores the intricate relationship between celebrities and the ideals of love and romance, dissecting how pop culture figures contribute to the evolving landscape of Valentine's Day trends. From the silver screen to social media platforms, we unravel the ways in which iconic figures redefine romantic ideals and inspire millions to aspire to a curated vision of love.

Celebrity Romance as a Spectacle: The world of pop culture is no stranger to the spectacle of celebrity romance, where the relationships of iconic figures are often thrust into the limelight. From Hollywood actors to chart-topping musicians, the public is captivated by the romantic lives of celebrities. This fascination extends beyond mere curiosity; it becomes a source of inspiration for millions, shaping societal perceptions of what constitutes an ideal romantic relationship.

Celebrities, often elevated to the status of cultural symbols, unintentionally become influencers in the realm of romance. The public dissects their relationships, scrutinizing gestures, public appearances, and social media posts for cues on what defines a successful and glamorous partnership. This phenomenon prompts reflection on how celebrity romance transcends mere gossip, becoming a cultural touchstone that influences the collective imagination and sets the stage for evolving romantic ideals.

Romantic Narratives in Film and Television: The silver screen has long been a canvas for painting romantic narratives, and celebrities embody characters that capture the hearts and fantasies of audiences worldwide. From classic Hollywood romances to contemporary streaming platforms, on-screen couples often transcend their fictional roles, becoming icons of love and romance. The impact of celebrity-led romantic narratives prompts reflection on how these stories seep into societal consciousness, influencing perceptions of what constitutes an ideal relationship.

The romantic narratives portrayed by celebrities in film and television shape not only individual preferences but also societal expectations. These narratives often reinforce traditional tropes while occasionally challenging established norms, contributing to an ever-evolving definition of romance. As we delve into the influence of romantic narratives, we uncover the ways in which celebrities contribute to reshaping the cultural landscape of love through the characters they portray.

Social Media as a Love Platform: In the digital age, the influence of celebrities on romantic ideals extends beyond the screen and onto the interactive realm of social media. Platforms like Instagram, Twitter, and TikTok offer celebrities a direct channel to share snippets of their personal lives, including romantic relationships. The curated nature of social media allows celebrities to craft and showcase idealized versions of their love stories, creating a visual narrative that resonates with millions of followers.

Social media platforms become not only a window into the private lives of celebrities but also a stage for the performance of romantic ideals. The carefully curated images, romantic declarations, and shared moments contribute to the construction of an aspirational love story. The impact of social media prompts reflection on how the digital landscape amplifies the influence of celebrities, transforming them into accessible influencers in the realm of romance.

Influence of Celebrity Relationships on Public Perceptions: The influence of pop culture icons on romantic ideals is particularly pronounced in how celebrity relationships shape public perceptions. As celebrities navigate the highs and lows of their love lives in the public eye, their experiences become fodder for societal discussions on love, commitment, and the nature of successful partnerships. The scrutiny of celebrity relationships prompts reflection on how public perceptions are molded by the often sensationalized narratives surrounding iconic figures.

Celebrities unintentionally become role models, with their relationships serving as templates for societal expectations. The impact of celebrity relationships on public perceptions prompts reflection on the fine line between reality and fantasy, as well as the responsibility that comes with being influential figures in the realm of romance. As we delve into the influence of celebrity relationships, we uncover the ways in which public perceptions of love are shaped and redefined by the actions and narratives of iconic figures.

Celebrity-Endorsed Brands in the Love Industry: The influence of celebrities extends beyond personal relationships and into the commercial realm, where celebrities often endorse brands related to love and romance. Whether it's fragrances, jewelry lines, or relationship advice books, celebrities become powerful influencers in shaping consumer behaviors and preferences in the love industry. The impact of celebrity endorsements prompts reflection on how the allure of celebrity relationships is commodified, creating a market where consumers aspire to emulate the romantic ideals associated with iconic figures.

Celebrity-endorsed brands not only capitalize on the public's fascination with celebrity romance but also actively contribute to the construction of romantic ideals. The association of a brand with a beloved celebrity couple elevates the product or service to more than a commodity; it becomes a symbol of the romantic narrative endorsed by these influential figures. As we delve into the influence of celebrity-endorsed brands, we uncover the ways in which iconic figures shape consumer choices and contribute to the perpetuation of romantic ideals in the market.

Impact of Social Media on Celebrity Romance: The advent of social media has redefined the nature of celebrity influence on romantic ideals, allowing for a direct and continuous connection between celebrities and their audience. The real-time sharing of moments, thoughts, and declarations of love on platforms like Instagram and Twitter contributes to the democratization of celebrity influence. The impact of social media on celebrity romance prompts reflection on how the immediacy of digital communication blurs the lines between the public and the private, creating a new paradigm for celebrity influence.

Social media platforms become platforms for the co-creation of celebrity narratives, with audiences actively participating in the construction and dissemination of romantic ideals. The instantaneous nature of social media allows celebrities to engage directly with their followers, creating a sense of intimacy that further amplifies their influence on public perceptions of love. As we delve into the impact of social media, we uncover the ways in which celebrities leverage these platforms to actively shape and participate in the ongoing discourse on romantic ideals.

Influence of Celebrity Breakups on Romantic Narratives: While the public is captivated by the spectacle of celebrity romance, the inevitable flip side is the fascination with celebrity breakups. The dissolution of iconic relationships often prompts societal reflection on the fragility of love, commitment, and the challenges that even the most glamorous partnerships face. The influence of celebrity breakups prompts reflection on how these publicized separations shape the narrative of romantic ideals, challenging preconceived notions and contributing to a more nuanced understanding of the complexities of love.

Celebrity breakups become teachable moments, allowing the public to witness the vulnerability of even the most seemingly perfect relationships. The impact of celebrity breakups prompts reflection on how these experiences contribute to the ongoing evolution of romantic ideals and reshape societal expectations. As we delve into the influence of celebrity breakups, we uncover the ways in which these publicized events become powerful narratives that redefine the discourse on love and resilience.

Challenges and Critiques of Celebrity Influence: While the influence of pop culture icons on romantic ideals is undeniable, it is not without its challenges and critiques. The idealized versions of love presented by celebrities often come under scrutiny for perpetuating unrealistic expectations and contributing to the commodification of romance. The challenges and critiques of celebrity influence prompt reflection on the responsibility that celebrities bear as inadvertent influencers in the realm of love.

Critics argue that the curated nature of celebrity relationships, often showcased on social media, creates an unrealistic standard that can lead to feelings of inadequacy and discontent among the public. The challenges and critiques of celebrity influence also extend to concerns about the impact of commodified love narratives on genuine human connections. As we delve into the complexities of celebrity influence, we uncover the nuanced conversations surrounding the responsibilities of celebrities and the impact of their narratives on societal perceptions of love.

In unraveling the influence of pop culture icons on romantic ideals, it becomes evident that celebrities play a multifaceted role in shaping the cultural narrative of love. From on-screen portrayals to real-life relationships, iconic figures become inadvertent influencers who contribute to the ongoing evolution of romantic ideals. Join us as we continue our exploration of the intersection between celebrity culture and Valentine's Day trends, delving into the ways in which iconic figures redefine the language of love and inspire millions to chase their own curated vision of romance.

Influence of Celebrity Relationships on Public Perceptions

In the ever-evolving landscape of modern romance, the influence of celebrity relationships on public perceptions stands as a testament to the power of pop culture icons to shape the way we view and understand love. This chapter delves into the intricate dynamics of how celebrity relationships become not just private affairs but cultural touchstones that influence public perceptions of love, commitment, and the idealized aspects of romantic partnerships.

Public Fascination with Celebrity Romance:

Celebrity relationships captivate the public imagination, transcending mere gossip to become cultural phenomena. The allure of glamorous partnerships, the intrigue surrounding high-profile weddings, and the fascination with the intricacies of celebrity love lives draw audiences into the world of iconic figures. This fascination goes beyond a mere curiosity about the personal lives of celebrities; it becomes a lens through which the public interprets and internalizes the dynamics of love and commitment.

As the public navigates the ups and downs of celebrity romances, it prompts reflection on how these relationships become aspirational templates for societal expectations. The public fascination with celebrity romance prompts exploration into the ways in which iconic figures unintentionally become influencers, shaping public perceptions and setting benchmarks for what constitutes an ideal romantic relationship.

The Role of Media in Shaping Narratives:

The media plays a pivotal role in shaping the narratives surrounding celebrity relationships, often turning these partnerships into ongoing sagas with their own story arcs. The constant coverage of celebrity romances through magazines, online articles, and entertainment news programs contributes to the creation of a narrative that goes beyond the surface-level details. Media framing influences not only how the public perceives celebrity relationships but also how they internalize and construct their own ideals of love.

The influence of media framing prompts reflection on the symbiotic relationship between celebrities and the outlets that cover their romantic lives. How does media framing contribute to the creation of narratives that influence public perceptions of love and commitment? What role does the constant scrutiny by the media play in shaping societal expectations related to iconic partnerships? As we explore the role of media in shaping narratives, we uncover the ways in which celebrity relationships become curated stories that permeate public consciousness.

Constructing Idealized Narratives:

Celebrity relationships often become platforms for the construction of idealized narratives that align with societal expectations of love. From fairytale weddings to grand gestures of affection, the curated nature of celebrity romances creates a storyline that is both aspirational and fantastical. This construction of idealized narratives prompts reflection on the impact of curated love stories on public perceptions and the expectations placed on real-life relationships.

The influence of constructed narratives prompts exploration into how celebrity relationships inadvertently contribute to the perpetuation of idealized versions of love. How do these idealized narratives influence public expectations of romantic gestures, commitment, and longevity in relationships? What role does the curated nature of celebrity relationships play in shaping the public's understanding of what constitutes a successful and glamorous partnership? As we delve into the construction of idealized narratives, we uncover the ways in which celebrity relationships become benchmarks for societal ideals of love.

Social Media as a Window into Celebrity Love Lives:

The advent of social media has transformed the way the public engages with celebrity relationships, offering an unfiltered and immediate view into the personal lives of iconic figures. Platforms like Instagram, Twitter, and TikTok allow celebrities to share intimate moments, declarations of love, and glimpses into their daily lives. The real-time nature of social media turns celebrity relationships into interactive experiences, where the public actively participates in the ongoing narrative.

The influence of social media prompts reflection on how the immediacy of digital communication blurs the lines between the public and the private, creating a new paradigm for celebrity influence. How do celebrities leverage social media to actively shape and participate in the ongoing discourse on romantic ideals? What impact does the interactive nature of social media have on the public's perception of celebrity relationships? As we explore the influence of social media, we uncover the ways in which the digital landscape transforms celebrity relationships into shared narratives that resonate with a global audience.

Impact of Celebrity Endorsements on Love-related Brands:

The influence of celebrities extends beyond personal relationships and into the commercial realm, where iconic figures often endorse brands related to love and romance. Fragrances, jewelry lines, and relationship advice books are among the myriad products that celebrities lend their names to, becoming powerful influencers in shaping consumer behaviors and preferences in the love industry. The impact of celebrity endorsements prompts exploration into how these endorsements contribute to the commodification of romantic ideals.

Celebrities endorsing love-related brands not only capitalize on the public's fascination with celebrity romance but also actively contribute to the construction of idealized versions of love. The association of a brand with a beloved celebrity couple elevates the product or service to more than a commodity; it becomes a symbol of the romantic narrative endorsed by these influential figures. As we delve into the impact of celebrity endorsements, we uncover the ways in which iconic figures shape consumer choices and contribute to the perpetuation of romantic ideals in the market.

Celebrity Relationships as Teachable Moments:

The public fascination with celebrity relationships extends to moments of vulnerability and heartbreak, creating what can be described as teachable moments in the realm of love. Celebrity breakups, in particular, become opportunities for the public to witness the challenges and complexities that even the most glamorous partnerships face. The impact of celebrity breakups prompts reflection on how these publicized separations become powerful narratives that redefine the discourse on love and resilience.

Celebrity relationships as teachable moments prompt exploration into how the public processes and internalizes the experiences of iconic figures. How do celebrity breakups influence public perceptions of the fragility of love and commitment? What role do these moments of vulnerability play in reshaping societal expectations related to the endurance of romantic partnerships? As we delve into celebrity relationships as teachable moments, we uncover the ways in which these experiences become integral components of the ongoing narrative surrounding love.

Challenges and Critiques of Celebrity Influence on Public Perceptions:

While the influence of celebrity relationships on public perceptions is profound, it is not without its challenges and critiques. The curated nature of celebrity romances, often showcased on social media and in the media, comes under scrutiny for perpetuating unrealistic expectations and contributing to the commodification of romance. The challenges and critiques prompt exploration into the nuanced conversations surrounding the responsibilities of celebrities as inadvertent influencers in the realm of love.

Critics argue that the idealized versions of love presented by celebrities create an unrealistic standard that can lead to feelings of inadequacy and discontent among the public. The challenges and critiques of celebrity influence also extend to concerns about the impact of commodified love narratives on genuine human connections. As we delve into the complexities of celebrity influence on public perceptions, we uncover the nuanced conversations surrounding the responsibilities of celebrities and the impact of their narratives on societal ideals of love.

In unraveling the influence of celebrity relationships on public perceptions, it becomes evident that celebrities play a multifaceted role in shaping the cultural narrative of love. From constructing idealized narratives to sharing vulnerable moments, iconic figures inadvertently become influencers who contribute to the ongoing evolution of societal ideals of romance. Join us as we continue our exploration of the intersection between celebrity culture and Valentine's Day trends, delving into the ways in which celebrity relationships redefine the language of love and inspire millions to navigate the complexities of modern romance.

Celebrity-Endorsed Brands in the Love Industry

In the intricate dance between celebrity culture and modern romance, the influence of pop culture icons extends beyond their personal relationships to the commercial realm. This chapter explores the phenomenon of celebrity-endorsed brands in the love industry, examining how iconic figures become influential players in shaping consumer behaviors, preferences, and the market dynamics of products associated with love and romance.

The Marriage of Celebrity and Commerce:

The marriage of celebrity and commerce has long been a symbiotic relationship, with iconic figures leveraging their influence to endorse a wide array of products. In the realm of the love industry, celebrities become powerful influencers, lending their names and personas to fragrances, jewelry lines, relationship advice books, and other products that promise to encapsulate the essence of love. This marriage of celebrity and commerce prompts exploration into how these endorsements contribute to the commodification of romantic ideals and the ways in which consumers navigate the intersection of fame and love.

As we delve into the influence of celebrity-endorsed brands in the love industry, we uncover the nuanced dynamics that define this relationship. How do celebrities become central figures in marketing campaigns for love-related products? What motivates consumers to gravitate towards products associated with iconic figures in the realm of love and romance? The exploration of this intersection offers insights into the evolving landscape where celebrity influence and consumerism converge.

Fragrances as Odes to Romance:

One of the prominent domains where celebrities leave their olfactory mark is the fragrance industry. Celebrity-endorsed perfumes often promise more than just a pleasant scent; they sell the allure of a curated love story, encapsulated in a bottle. Fragrances become olfactory expressions of the romantic ideals associated with the celebrity figure, offering consumers a chance to embody a piece of the star's love narrative. The influence of celebrity-endorsed fragrances prompts exploration into the ways in which scents become powerful carriers of romantic narratives and how consumers engage with these olfactory tales.

How do celebrities collaborate with perfumers to craft fragrances that align with their romantic personas? What role do marketing strategies play in presenting these scents as more than just products but as gateways to an aspirational love experience? The exploration of fragrances as odes to romance unravels the artistry and intentionality behind the creation of celebrity-endorsed scents and the impact these olfactory stories have on consumer perceptions of love.

Jewelry Lines: Adorning Love with Celebrity Sparkle:

Celebrities often extend their influence to the realm of jewelry, collaborating with designers to create signature lines that embody their interpretation of love. These jewelry lines, adorned with the sparkle of celebrity endorsement, offer consumers the chance to wear a tangible symbol of the romantic ideals associated with the iconic figure. The influence of celebrity-endorsed jewelry lines prompts exploration into the ways in which accessories become not just adornments but carriers of the romantic narratives crafted by iconic figures.

How do celebrities infuse their personal love stories, values, or symbols into the design and concept of their jewelry lines? What emotions and aspirations do these accessories evoke in consumers who seek to align themselves with the romantic ideals associated with the celebrity figure? As we delve into jewelry lines adorned with celebrity sparkle, we unravel the intricate dance between the tangible expressions of love and the intangible allure of fame.

Relationship Advice Books: Wisdom from the Stars:

The world of celebrity-endorsed brands in the love industry extends beyond tangible products to include the wisdom imparted through relationship advice books. Celebrities, often unintentionally thrust into the role of relationship gurus, share their insights, experiences, and reflections on love, commitment, and navigating the complexities of romantic partnerships. These books, carrying the weight of celebrity endorsement, become guides for consumers seeking to understand and emulate the romantic ideals associated with the iconic figure.

How do celebrities transition from personal experiences to offering relationship advice to a broad audience? What role do these books play in shaping public perceptions of love, and how do consumers navigate the line between celebrity narratives and real-world relationship dynamics? The exploration of relationship advice books delves into the ways in which iconic figures become inadvertent counselors, influencing the perspectives and choices of their readers.

Impact on Consumer Behaviors and Preferences:

The influence of celebrity-endorsed brands in the love industry extends beyond individual products to shape broader consumer behaviors and preferences. The allure of products associated with iconic figures often goes beyond functionality, tapping into the emotional and aspirational aspects of love.

This impact on consumer behaviors prompts exploration into how the market dynamics of love-related products are influenced by the intersection of celebrity culture and consumerism.

How do consumers navigate the decision-making process when choosing products endorsed by celebrities in the love industry? What role do emotions, aspirations, and the desire to align with romantic ideals play in shaping consumer preferences? The exploration of impact on consumer behaviors and preferences unravels the complex interplay between celebrity influence, market dynamics, and the emotional resonance that love-related products carry for consumers.

Challenges and Ethical Considerations:

While the marriage of celebrity and commerce in the love industry presents lucrative opportunities, it is not without its challenges and ethical considerations. The commodification of romantic ideals through celebrity endorsements raises questions about authenticity, transparency, and the potential exploitation of genuine emotions for commercial gain. The challenges and ethical considerations prompt exploration into the responsibility that celebrities, marketers, and consumers bear in navigating the fine line between aspirational narratives and ethical practices.

How do celebrities balance the commercial aspect of endorsing love-related products with the authenticity of their personal narratives? What ethical considerations should marketers and brands keep in mind when leveraging celebrity endorsements in the love industry? The exploration of challenges and ethical considerations offers a critical lens through which to assess the impact of the celebrity-endorsed brands on both the industry and the consumers they target.

The Future Landscape of Celebrity-Endorsed Brands in the Love Industry:

As the dynamics of celebrity culture, consumerism, and love continue to evolve, the future landscape of celebrity-endorsed brands in the love industry holds both opportunities and challenges. The trajectory of this intersection prompts exploration into emerging trends, evolving consumer expectations, and the ways in which celebrities and brands adapt to the shifting landscape. The exploration of the future landscape offers insights into the continued influence of iconic figures on the market dynamics of love-related products.

How will the evolution of celebrity culture impact the types of love-related products that gain prominence in the market? What role will authenticity and transparency play in the future landscape of celebrity endorsements in the love industry? As we explore the future landscape, we unravel the potential trajectories that will shape the ongoing dance between celebrity influence and consumer choices in the realm of modern romance.

In navigating the world of celebrity-endorsed brands in the love industry, it becomes evident that the intersection of fame and love creates a complex and dynamic space. From fragrances to jewelry lines and relationship advice books, iconic figures inadvertently become influencers in the market dynamics of products associated with love and romance. Join us as we continue our exploration of the interplay between celebrity culture and Valentine's Day trends, delving into the ways in which celebrities shape not only personal narratives but also the commercial landscape of love.

Impact of Social Media on Celebrity Romance

In the era of digital connectivity, the influence of celebrity relationships extends beyond traditional media to the interactive and immediate realm of social media. This chapter explores the impact of social media on celebrity romance, unraveling how platforms like Instagram, Twitter, and TikTok transform the dynamics of love narratives, engagement with fans, and the very nature of the public-private divide in the lives of iconic figures.

The Rise of the Social Media Love Story:

Social media platforms have become stages for the public performance of celebrity relationships, transforming love stories into interactive experiences for millions of followers. From Instagram posts capturing intimate moments to Twitter threads of affectionate exchanges, celebrities leverage social media to curate and share their love narratives directly with the public. The rise of the social media love story prompts exploration into how iconic figures navigate the balance between authenticity and curation in presenting their romantic relationships to a global audience.

How have social media platforms become integral to the storytelling of celebrity romances? What role does the visual nature of platforms like Instagram play in shaping the narrative of love and commitment? As we delve into the rise of the social media love story, we uncover the ways in which celebrities become active participants in shaping the discourse on modern romance through their curated online personas.

Direct Engagement with Fans:

Social media provides a direct channel for celebrities to engage with their fans, offering glimpses into their personal lives and creating a sense of intimacy. Platforms like Instagram allow celebrities to share not only carefully curated images but also unfiltered moments, fostering a connection with fans that transcends the boundaries of traditional media. The direct engagement with fans prompts exploration into the ways in which social media platforms democratize access to celebrity narratives and redefine the relationship between public figures and their audience.

How does the interactive nature of social media transform the dynamic between celebrities and their fans? What impact does direct engagement, including responding to comments and sharing personal anecdotes, have on the perception of celebrity relationships? The exploration of direct engagement with fans unravels the ways in which social media platforms become bridges connecting iconic figures with their global audience.

Real-Time Narratives and Instantaneous Updates:

Social media's real-time nature allows celebrities to provide instantaneous updates on their lives, creating a continuous narrative that unfolds alongside real-world events. From sharing moments of celebration to posting about challenges, celebrities use platforms like Twitter to offer unfiltered glimpses into their daily lives. The real-time narratives and instantaneous updates prompt exploration into how social media becomes a dynamic space where the boundaries between public and private are blurred, and where love stories are narrated in sync with the rhythm of everyday life.

How do celebrities navigate the balance between sharing spontaneous moments and maintaining a curated online presence? What impact does the immediacy of social media updates have on public perceptions of the authenticity of celebrity relationships? The exploration of real-time narratives and instantaneous updates unravels the ways in which social media platforms become living canvases for the unfolding stories of love.

Visual Language of Love:

Social media platforms, particularly visual-centric ones like Instagram, introduce a unique visual language through which celebrities communicate their love narratives. From carefully posed couple photos to shared travel experiences, the visual language of love on social media becomes a powerful tool for conveying emotions and crafting a romantic narrative. The exploration of this visual language prompts reflection on how iconic figures utilize images to construct an aspirational vision of love and intimacy.

How do celebrities curate and compose visual narratives that align with societal expectations of romance? What role does aesthetic cohesion play in shaping the visual language of love on social media? As we delve into the visual language of love, we uncover the ways in which images become potent carriers of emotions and narratives in the digital landscape.

Challenges of Living in the Public Eye:

While social media offers a platform for celebrities to share their love stories, it also exposes them to the challenges of living in the public eye. The constant scrutiny of their relationships, comments from followers, and the potential for online criticism create a unique set of pressures. The challenges of living in the public eye prompt exploration into the impact of social media on the mental and emotional well-being of iconic figures navigating the complexities of modern romance.

How do celebrities cope with the pressures and challenges of sharing personal moments on a public platform?

What strategies do they employ to maintain boundaries while still engaging with their audience? The exploration of the challenges of living in the public eye offers insights into the delicate balance that celebrities must strike as they navigate the fine line between public personas and private lives.

Constructing Authenticity in a Curated Space:

The tension between authenticity and curation becomes particularly pronounced in the realm of social media, where celebrities walk a tightrope between sharing genuine moments and maintaining a polished online presence. The construction of authenticity in a curated space prompts exploration into how iconic figures navigate the expectations of transparency while still preserving elements of privacy. Social media becomes a stage where celebrities not only share their love stories but also actively participate in shaping the discourse on what constitutes an authentic portrayal of modern romance.

How do celebrities balance the desire for authenticity with the pressures of maintaining a certain image? What impact does the curated nature of social media have on public perceptions of the genuine nature of celebrity relationships? The exploration of constructing authenticity in a curated space unravels the complexities of navigating the authenticity paradox in the digital age.

Navigating Challenges and Controversies:

The immediacy of social media also means that celebrities must navigate challenges and controversies in real-time. From addressing rumors to responding to public critiques, iconic figures use platforms like Twitter to shape the narrative surrounding their relationships. Navigating challenges and controversies prompts exploration into the ways in which social media becomes a tool for managing public perception, addressing controversies, and even reshaping the narrative of love in the face of adversity.

How do celebrities strategically use social media to address challenges and controversies? What impact does this real-time engagement have on public perceptions and the overall narrative surrounding their relationships? The exploration of navigating challenges and controversies offers insights into the evolving strategies that celebrities employ to maintain control over their love stories in the digital age.

The Evolution of Relationship Milestones:

Social media platforms have also transformed traditional relationship milestones into shareable moments that become part of the public narrative. From announcements of new relationships to declarations of love on anniversaries, iconic figures use social media to curate and share significant moments with their audience. The evolution of relationship milestones prompts exploration into how social media platforms redefine the very concept of milestones in the context of modern romance.

How do celebrities utilize social media to share relationship milestones, and what impact does this have on public engagement with their love stories? What role do public reactions play in shaping the narrative surrounding relationship milestones in the digital age? The exploration of the evolution of relationship milestones unravels the ways in which social media platforms become integral to the construction of a shared love narrative.

Global Impact and Cultural Influence:

Social media platforms transcend geographical boundaries, allowing celebrity relationships to have a global impact and cultural influence. The narratives of iconic figures reach audiences around the world, shaping not only individual perceptions but also contributing to a broader cultural conversation about love and romance. The global impact and cultural influence prompt exploration into how social media platforms become conduits for the transmission of cultural norms, ideals, and evolving perspectives on modern romance.

How do celebrities navigate the responsibility of being cultural influencers in the context of love and relationships? What impact does the global reach of social media have on the cultural dynamics surrounding love narratives? The exploration of global impact and cultural influence unravels the ways in which social media transforms celebrity relationships into cultural touchpoints that resonate with diverse audiences.

Privacy and Boundaries in the Digital Age:

The blurring of public and private spheres on social media prompts reflection on the concept of privacy and the boundaries that celebrities seek to establish in the digital age. The constant visibility afforded by these platforms raises questions about the right to personal space, the impact on personal relationships, and the challenges of maintaining a semblance of normalcy in the midst of a curated online presence. Privacy and boundaries in the digital age prompt exploration into the ways in which celebrities navigate the delicate balance between openness and personal space in sharing their love narratives.

How do celebrities define and communicate their boundaries on social media platforms? What impact does the constant visibility have on their personal lives and relationships? The exploration of privacy and boundaries in the digital age offers insights into the evolving dynamics of celebrity relationships in the era of constant connectivity.

Fan Engagement and Fandom Culture:

Social media platforms not only facilitate direct engagement with fans but also give rise to a vibrant culture of fandom that actively participates in the love narratives of iconic figures. Fan engagement and fandom culture prompt exploration into the ways in which social media becomes a space for fans to express support, celebrate relationship milestones, and actively contribute to the construction of the narrative surrounding celebrity romance.

How do fans engage with and contribute to the love stories presented by celebrities on social media? What impact does fan culture have on the overall perception and longevity of celebrity relationships? The exploration of fan engagement and fandom culture unravels the symbiotic relationship between iconic figures and their global audience, shaping the narrative of modern romance in real-time.

In unraveling the impact of social media on celebrity romance, it becomes evident that these platforms redefine not only how love stories are told but also how they are experienced by a global audience. From direct engagement with fans to the challenges of living in the public eye, social media platforms become dynamic spaces where iconic figures actively shape the discourse on modern romance. Join us as we continue our exploration of the interplay between celebrity culture and Valentine's Day trends, delving into the ways in which social media transforms love narratives in the digital age.

Chapter 4: Virtual Celebrations and Long-Distance Love

Navigating Love Across Time Zones

In the age of interconnectedness, the dynamics of love have transcended geographical boundaries. Long-distance relationships have become not just a challenge but a testament to the resilience and adaptability of modern love. This chapter explores the nuances of navigating love across time zones, delving into the intricacies, challenges, and unique joys that come with maintaining a romantic connection when miles apart.

The Globalization of Love:

Love, once confined to local communities and familiar settings, has now embraced a globalized dimension. People from different corners of the world can connect and form romantic relationships, transcending physical distances. The globalization of love prompts exploration into the ways in which individuals navigate cultural nuances, time zone disparities, and the challenges of building connections with someone who may be thousands of miles away.

How does the globalization of love impact the diversity of relationship experiences? What role do cultural differences play in shaping the dynamics of long-distance relationships? As we delve into the intricacies of navigating love across time zones, we uncover the ways in which the global landscape has redefined the boundaries of romantic connections.

Challenges of Time Zone Disparities:

One of the central challenges of long-distance love is the significant time zone disparities that can create a temporal barrier between partners. The challenges of time zone disparities prompt exploration into the strategies couples employ to coordinate communication, share moments, and maintain a sense of connection despite being in different parts of the world.

How do couples navigate the logistical challenges of coordinating schedules across different time zones? What impact do time zone disparities have on the frequency and quality of communication in long-distance relationships? The exploration of challenges related to time zone disparities unravels the ways in which couples innovate and adapt to bridge the temporal gap in their romantic journey.

Communication Strategies for Global Love:

Communication lies at the heart of any relationship, and in the context of long-distance love across time zones, it becomes even more crucial. Partners must navigate through the challenges of asynchronous communication, varying daily routines, and the need for intentional efforts to stay connected. The communication strategies for global love prompt exploration into how couples negotiate the digital landscape to foster emotional intimacy and sustain a sense of togetherness.

What communication tools and platforms do couples rely on to bridge the gap created by time zone differences? How do partners develop unique communication rituals that accommodate their respective schedules and locations? The exploration of communication strategies for global love unveils the ways in which couples utilize technology to overcome distance and maintain a meaningful connection.

Embracing the Joys of Global Connections:

While long-distance relationships may present challenges, they also offer unique joys and opportunities. Embracing the joys of global connections prompts exploration into the ways in which couples find delight in cultural exchange, shared experiences across continents, and the richness that diversity brings to their romantic journey.

How do partners celebrate and incorporate each other's cultural backgrounds into their relationship? What role do shared virtual experiences play in fostering a sense of togetherness despite the physical distance? The exploration of embracing the joys of global connections uncovers the ways in which long-distance couples find strength and joy in the unique aspects of their cross-cultural love stories.

Technology as the Bridge Across Miles:

Technology serves as the lifeline for couples navigating love across time zones. From video calls to instant messaging, technology becomes the bridge that transcends physical distances and allows partners to stay virtually connected. The role of technology as the bridge across miles prompts exploration into the ways in which couples leverage digital tools to bridge the gap between them and create a sense of shared presence.

How do couples use technology to share everyday moments and maintain a sense of closeness despite the physical distance? What impact does the visual and auditory dimension of technology have on the emotional connection between partners? The exploration of technology as the bridge across miles unveils the ways in which the digital landscape becomes a vital component of the modern long-distance relationship.

Creating Shared Virtual Spaces:

Long-distance couples often find solace in creating shared virtual spaces that serve as a surrogate for physical togetherness. From virtual date nights to shared playlists and online games, these spaces become avenues for shared experiences that contribute to the richness of the relationship.

Creating shared virtual spaces prompts exploration into the ways in which couples craft a sense of belonging and shared identity in the digital realm.

What virtual activities do long-distance couples engage in to create a sense of shared presence? How do these shared virtual spaces contribute to the emotional bond between partners? The exploration of creating shared virtual spaces unveils the ways in which couples actively participate in the construction of a digital environment that mirrors the intimacy of physical togetherness.

Celebrating Milestones from Afar:

Milestones in a relationship are often marked by physical proximity, but long-distance couples must navigate the celebration of these significant moments from afar. Whether it's anniversaries, birthdays, or other special occasions, celebrating milestones from afar prompts exploration into the creative ways couples find to make these moments memorable and meaningful despite the distance.

How do partners celebrate milestones in a virtual space, and what role do digital surprises and gifts play in creating a sense of celebration? How do couples navigate the emotional challenges of not being physically present for important moments? The exploration of celebrating milestones from afar unveils the ways in which long-distance couples infuse creativity and thoughtfulness into their virtual celebrations.

Overcoming the Emotional Distance:

Beyond the physical separation, long-distance relationships often require partners to navigate emotional distances that may arise due to time zone disparities, cultural differences, or the challenges of asynchronous communication. Overcoming the emotional distance prompts exploration into the ways in which couples actively work towards maintaining emotional intimacy, trust, and a deep connection despite the physical miles between them.

How do partners address emotional challenges that may arise in long-distance relationships, and what role does open communication play in overcoming misunderstandings? What strategies do couples employ to build and sustain trust when separated by time zones? The exploration of overcoming emotional distance unveils the emotional intelligence and resilience that long-distance couples develop as they navigate the complexities of their romantic journey.

Building a Future Together:

Long-distance couples often face the question of building a future together despite the physical separation. The prospect of eventually closing the distance prompts exploration into the ways in which couples plan for a shared future, navigate the complexities of relocation, and envision a life where time zone disparities are no longer a factor.

How do partners discuss and plan for a future where they can be physically together? What role does mutual commitment and shared goals play in sustaining a long-distance relationship with the intention of eventually closing the gap? The exploration of building a future together unveils the ways in which long-distance couples actively work towards a shared vision that transcends geographical boundaries.

Learning and Growth in Long-Distance Love:

Long-distance relationships, despite their challenges, offer opportunities for profound learning and growth. Partners must develop strong communication skills, foster trust, and navigate cultural differences, contributing to personal development and resilience. The learning and growth in long-distance love prompt exploration into the ways in which individuals and couples evolve as they navigate the complexities of maintaining a romantic connection across time zones.

What lessons do individuals glean from the challenges and joys of long-distance love, and how does this contribute to personal growth? How do couples navigate the evolution of their relationship over time and embrace the changes that come with the progression of their romantic journey? The exploration of learning and growth in long-distance love unveils the transformative potential that these relationships hold for those who embark on this unique path.

In navigating love across time zones, it becomes evident that distance, whether physical or temporal, does not diminish the depth and intensity of romantic connections. Instead, long-distance relationships become a testament to the adaptability and resilience of modern love, demonstrating that the bonds formed across miles can be as profound and enduring as those forged in close proximity. Join us as we continue our exploration of virtual celebrations and long-distance love, delving into the diverse ways in which couples navigate the complexities and joys of modern romance.

Virtual Celebrations and Shared Online Experiences

In the digital age, the landscape of romantic celebrations has expanded beyond physical proximity, allowing couples in long-distance relationships to share meaningful experiences through virtual means. This chapter explores the realm of virtual celebrations and shared online experiences, delving into the creative ways couples bridge the gap and make special moments memorable despite the physical distance.

Redesigning Celebrations for the Digital Realm:

Celebrations, whether birthdays, anniversaries, or other special occasions, are traditionally associated with physical presence and shared experiences. In the context of long-distance love, partners must redesign these celebrations for the digital realm, leveraging technology to create virtual spaces where the essence of the moment can be shared. This prompts exploration into the ways in which couples adapt and innovate to infuse virtual celebrations with the same joy and significance as in-person gatherings.

How do couples reimagine the elements of traditional celebrations to fit the digital landscape? What role does creativity play in designing virtual spaces that capture the essence of special occasions? The exploration of redesigning celebrations for the digital realm unveils the ways in which couples transform distance into an opportunity for inventive and personalized celebrations.

Virtual Date Nights:

Date nights, a cornerstone of romantic connections, take on a digital twist in long-distance relationships. Virtual date nights become a way for couples to share quality time, engage in shared activities, and create a sense of togetherness despite the physical miles. The exploration of virtual date nights prompts an investigation into the various activities and platforms couples utilize to craft memorable digital experiences that contribute to the emotional closeness between partners.

How do couples coordinate and plan virtual date nights that cater to their unique interests and preferences? What impact does the virtual setting have on the dynamics of these shared activities, and how do partners foster a sense of presence despite the physical separation? The exploration of virtual date nights unravels the ways in which couples actively invest in the quality of their digital interactions to enhance the depth of their connection.

Online Games and Shared Hobbies:

The digital realm offers a plethora of opportunities for couples to engage in shared hobbies and playful activities, transcending geographical distances. Online games, collaborative projects, and shared hobbies become avenues for couples to bond, laugh, and create shared memories. The exploration of online games and shared hobbies prompts an inquiry into the types of activities couples find most engaging, the platforms they utilize, and the impact of these shared experiences on the fabric of their relationship.

What role do online games and shared hobbies play in fostering a sense of camaraderie and shared achievement? How do couples navigate the challenges and joys of participating in activities that require coordination and cooperation across time zones? The exploration of online games and shared hobbies unveils the ways in which couples leverage the digital landscape to weave threads of shared experiences into the tapestry of their relationship.

Virtual Movie Nights and Music Sessions:

The world of entertainment takes center stage in virtual celebrations, with couples creating shared experiences around movies, music, and other forms of artistic expression. Virtual movie nights and music sessions become rituals through which partners can enjoy cultural experiences together, share reactions, and immerse themselves in the creative world. The exploration of virtual movie nights and music sessions prompts an examination of the role of entertainment in fostering emotional connections and the ways in which couples use these experiences to enrich their relationship.

How do couples curate virtual movie nights and music sessions that align with their shared tastes and preferences? What impact does the shared enjoyment of cultural experiences have on the emotional resonance of the relationship? The exploration of virtual movie nights and music sessions unveils the ways in which couples utilize the arts as a conduit for shared emotions and cultural intimacy.

Digital Memory-Making:

Capturing and preserving memories is an integral part of any relationship, and in the context of long-distance love, the digital landscape becomes a canvas for creating and revisiting shared moments. Digital memory-making encompasses the creation of photo albums, collaborative online journals, and other virtual artifacts that serve as tangible reminders of the journey traveled together. The exploration of digital memory-making delves into the ways in which couples craft a narrative of their relationship through digital means, curating a collection of moments that transcend the physical distance.

How do couples use digital platforms to document their journey, and what role does the act of memory-making play in reinforcing the emotional bond between partners? How do virtual artifacts become touchstones that anchor the relationship in shared experiences and milestones? The exploration of digital memory-making unveils the ways in which couples actively contribute to the construction of a shared narrative that transcends the limitations of physical separation.

Online Gift-Giving and Surprises:

The act of giving and receiving gifts takes on new dimensions in the digital age, with couples in long-distance relationships leveraging online platforms to express affection and thoughtfulness. Online gift-giving and surprises become gestures through which partners can bridge the physical gap, infusing the relationship with tangible tokens of love. The exploration of online gift-giving and surprises prompts an investigation into the types of gifts couples exchange, the thought processes behind these gestures, and the impact of virtual surprises on the emotional connection between partners.

How do couples navigate the process of selecting and sending gifts online, and what significance do these gestures hold in the context of long-distance love? What role does surprise play in keeping the relationship dynamic and full of anticipation? The exploration of online gift-giving and surprises unveils the ways in which couples use virtual platforms to express love and create moments of delight.

Online Celebrations of Milestones:

Milestones in a relationship, whether it's the anniversary of the day they met or other significant moments, are cause for celebration. In the digital landscape, partners find creative ways to mark these milestones with online parties, virtual gatherings with friends, and collaborative projects that commemorate the journey traveled together. The exploration of online celebrations of milestones delves into the ways in which couples transform significant moments into opportunities for shared joy, reflection, and connection.

How do couples plan and execute online celebrations that capture the essence of significant milestones? What impact do virtual gatherings with friends and family have on the sense of community and shared support within the relationship? The exploration of online celebrations of milestones unveils the ways in which couples use the digital space to amplify the joy and significance of special occasions.

Fostering Connection Through Video Calls:

Video calls, a staple in long-distance relationships, become integral to virtual celebrations, offering a real-time connection that transcends the limitations of text-based communication. Fostering connection through video calls prompts an examination of the role of visual and auditory cues in maintaining a sense of presence and intimacy, even when partners are physically separated by vast distances.

How do couples navigate the challenges and joys of video calls as a primary mode of communication? What impact does the visual dimension of video calls have on the emotional connection between partners, and how do couples actively use this medium to nurture their bond? The exploration of fostering connection through video calls unveils the ways in which technology becomes a conduit for sustaining the visual and emotional intimacy that is essential for the well-being of long-distance relationships.

Building a Virtual Community:

The digital landscape not only facilitates one-on-one interactions but also provides opportunities for couples to build a virtual community around their relationship. Online forums, social media groups, and other digital platforms become spaces where couples can connect with others in similar situations, share advice, and foster a sense of belonging. Building a virtual community prompts exploration into the ways in which couples actively participate in the broader digital ecosystem, contributing to and drawing support from a network of individuals who understand the unique challenges and joys of long-distance love.

How do couples engage with online communities, and what impact does this virtual support system have on their resilience and well-being? What role does shared experience play in fostering connections within the broader community of long-distance couples? The exploration of building a virtual community unveils the ways in which couples contribute to the collective wisdom and camaraderie that defines the digital landscape of long-distance relationships.

In the realm of virtual celebrations and shared online experiences, distance becomes an opportunity for creativity, innovation, and the deepening of emotional connections. Couples in long-distance relationships actively leverage the digital landscape to create moments of joy, surprise, and shared intimacy that contribute to the resilience and vibrancy of their connection. Join us as we continue our exploration of virtual celebrations and long-distance love, delving into the diverse ways in which couples navigate the complexities and joys of modern romance.

Challenges and Joys of Long-Distance Relationships

Long-distance relationships, while marked by unique challenges, also hold profound joys that stem from the resilience, commitment, and creativity of the individuals involved. This chapter explores the multifaceted landscape of long-distance relationships, shedding light on the challenges faced and the joys discovered in navigating love across miles.

The Challenge of Physical Separation:

Perhaps the most evident challenge in a long-distance relationship is the physical separation that requires partners to exist in different geographical locations. The challenge of physical separation prompts exploration into the ways in which individuals navigate the longing for physical closeness, the impact on daily routines, and the emotional toll of not being able to share the same physical space.

How do partners cope with the challenge of physical separation, and what strategies do they employ to feel connected despite the distance? What impact does the absence of shared physical experiences have on the emotional dynamics of the relationship? The exploration of the challenge of physical separation unveils the ways in which couples actively work towards maintaining a sense of togetherness despite being physically apart.

Time Zone Disparities and Communication Challenges:

Long-distance relationships often involve partners living in different time zones, creating a significant challenge in coordinating communication and shared activities. Time zone disparities and communication challenges prompt exploration into the strategies couples employ to bridge the temporal gap, the impact on the frequency and quality of communication, and the need for intentional efforts to stay connected across different time zones.

How do partners navigate the logistical challenges of coordinating schedules when living in different time zones? What role does asynchronous communication play in maintaining a sense of connection, and how do couples adapt to the ebb and flow of time zone differences? The exploration of time zone disparities and communication challenges unravels the ways in which couples actively engage in intentional communication to overcome the constraints of distance.

Coping with Loneliness and Emotional Distance:

The physical and temporal separation inherent in long-distance relationships can give rise to feelings of loneliness and emotional distance. Coping with loneliness and emotional distance prompts exploration into the emotional toll of being physically apart, the strategies couples use to address feelings of isolation, and the importance of open communication in navigating the complexities of emotional distance.

How do partners cope with feelings of loneliness, and what role does emotional communication play in bridging the emotional gap? What impact does the awareness of physical separation have on the overall emotional well-being of individuals in long-distance relationships? The exploration of coping with loneliness and emotional distance unveils the ways in which couples actively address the emotional challenges that arise in the absence of physical proximity.

Trust and Insecurity Across Distances:

Trust becomes a cornerstone in long-distance relationships, as partners must rely on faith in each other's commitment and fidelity. However, the physical separation can also give rise to feelings of insecurity and doubt. Trust and insecurity across distances prompt exploration into the factors that contribute to building and sustaining trust, the challenges of managing insecurities, and the role of open communication in fostering a secure emotional connection.

How do partners actively nurture trust, and what strategies do they employ to address feelings of insecurity that may arise in the absence of physical presence? What impact does open communication have on building a foundation of trust that withstands the challenges of distance? The exploration of trust and insecurity across distances unveils the ways in which couples actively work towards maintaining a strong and secure connection despite the physical miles between them.

Balancing Independence and Togetherness:

Long-distance relationships often require individuals to strike a delicate balance between maintaining independence and fostering togetherness. The challenge of balancing independence and togetherness prompts exploration into how partners navigate individual pursuits, shared goals, and the importance of creating a relationship dynamic that accommodates both autonomy and connection.

How do couples balance the desire for personal growth and independence with the need for shared experiences and a sense of togetherness? What role do individual goals and aspirations play in shaping the dynamics of long-distance relationships? The exploration of balancing independence and togetherness unveils the ways in which couples actively negotiate the complexities of maintaining individual identities within the context of a committed partnership.

Uncertainty About the Future:

Long-distance relationships often come with an inherent uncertainty about the future, including questions about when the physical distance will be closed, potential changes in life circumstances, and the evolution of the relationship over time. The uncertainty about the future prompts exploration into how couples discuss and plan for the next steps, the challenges of navigating ambiguity, and the importance of aligning future goals within the relationship.

How do partners address and manage uncertainties about the future, and what role does open communication play in facilitating discussions about long-term plans? How do couples navigate potential changes in life circumstances and the impact of these changes on the trajectory of the relationship? The exploration of uncertainty about the future unveils the ways in which couples actively engage in dialogue and strategic planning to shape the path ahead.

Celebrating Milestones from Afar:

While celebrating milestones is an essential part of any relationship, long-distance couples face the unique challenge of commemorating significant moments from afar. The challenge of celebrating milestones prompts exploration into the creative ways couples find to make these moments memorable and meaningful despite the physical distance.

How do couples navigate the process of planning and executing virtual celebrations that capture the essence of significant milestones? What impact does the absence of physical presence have on the emotional dynamics of celebrating important moments? The exploration of celebrating milestones from afar unveils the ways in which couples actively infuse creativity and thoughtfulness into their virtual celebrations, turning challenges into opportunities for shared joy.

Personal Growth and Independence:

Amidst the challenges, long-distance relationships also offer opportunities for personal growth and the cultivation of independence. The joys of personal growth and independence prompt exploration into the ways in which individuals develop resilience, self-reliance, and a sense of identity within the context of a long-distance relationship.

How do individuals navigate the journey of personal growth within the constraints of physical separation, and what role does the relationship play in shaping individual identities? What joys and discoveries emerge from the pursuit of personal goals and aspirations while in a long-distance partnership? The exploration of personal growth and independence unveils the ways in which individuals actively embrace the opportunities for self-discovery and development that arise in the unique landscape of long-distance love.

Rediscovering Intimacy in Digital Spaces:

Long-distance relationships challenge couples to rediscover intimacy in digital spaces, leveraging technology to create emotional closeness despite the physical miles. The joys of rediscovering intimacy in digital spaces prompt exploration into the ways in which partners use technology to nurture emotional connection, share vulnerable moments, and foster a sense of closeness that transcends the limitations of physical separation.

How do couples actively engage in acts of digital intimacy, and what impact does this rediscovery have on the emotional depth of the relationship? What joys emerge from the creative ways couples use technology to bridge the gap between them and create shared moments of intimacy? The exploration of rediscovering intimacy in digital spaces unveils the ways in which couples actively contribute to the evolution of modern romance within the context of long-distance love.

The Joy of Reunion and Shared Physical Presence:

One of the most anticipated joys in a long-distance relationship is the moment of reunion, where partners can finally share the same physical space after a period of separation. The joy of reunion and shared physical presence prompts exploration into the emotional dynamics of coming together, the significance of physical closeness, and the ways in which couples celebrate the joy of being in each other's arms again.

How do partners navigate the emotional highs of reunion, and what rituals and shared activities mark the joyous occasion of being physically together? What impact does the joy of reunion have on the overall resilience and vibrancy of the relationship? The exploration of the joy of reunion and shared physical presence unveils the ways in which couples actively savor the moments of togetherness that follow periods of physical separation.

In navigating the challenges and joys of long-distance relationships, individuals and couples actively contribute to the evolution of modern love. The resilience, creativity, and commitment exhibited in overcoming challenges and embracing moments of joy paint a vivid picture of the adaptability of contemporary romance. Join us as we continue our exploration of virtual celebrations and long-distance love, delving into the diverse ways in which couples navigate the complexities and joys of modern romance.

Technology's Role in Sustaining Long-Distance Love

Long-distance relationships have undergone a transformative shift in the digital age, with technology serving as a crucial lifeline that sustains and enriches romantic connections across vast distances. This chapter explores the multifaceted role of technology in sustaining long-distance love, delving into the ways in which digital tools and platforms become conduits for communication, emotional intimacy, and shared experiences.

Digital Communication:

At the heart of long-distance relationships lies digital communication, a dynamic and versatile tool that enables partners to bridge the physical gap and maintain a constant flow of connection. The role of digital communication in sustaining long-distance love prompts exploration into the various platforms and channels couples utilize, the impact of instant messaging and video calls on relationship dynamics, and the ways in which partners navigate the nuances of virtual interaction.

How do couples use digital communication to stay connected on a daily basis, and what role does the immediacy of instant messaging play in fostering a sense of presence? What impact does video calling have on the emotional connection between partners, and how do couples navigate the challenges of expressing emotions through digital means? The exploration of digital communication unveils the ways in which technology becomes the primary conduit for maintaining a vibrant and constant connection in long-distance relationships.

Virtual Presence Through Video Calls:

Video calls emerge as a cornerstone of virtual presence in long-distance relationships, offering partners the ability to see and hear each other in real-time. The role of video calls in sustaining long-distance love prompts exploration into the ways in which partners utilize visual and auditory cues to create a sense of shared presence, the impact of video calls on emotional intimacy, and the rituals that couples develop around virtual face-to-face interactions.

How do partners integrate video calls into their daily routines, and what significance does the visual dimension of this technology have on the emotional dynamics of the relationship? What rituals and activities do couples engage in during video calls to foster a sense of togetherness despite the physical distance? The exploration of virtual presence through video calls unveils the ways in which couples actively leverage technology to create moments of shared intimacy and connection.

The Digital Landscape of Emotional Intimacy:

Technology plays a pivotal role in shaping the emotional landscape of long-distance relationships, with partners relying on digital platforms to express love, share vulnerabilities, and cultivate emotional intimacy. The role of the digital landscape in emotional intimacy prompts exploration into the ways in which couples navigate the challenges of expressing emotions through text and multimedia, the impact of virtual gestures on the emotional bond, and the creative ways partners use technology to deepen their emotional connection.

How do couples convey emotions through digital means, and what strategies do they employ to ensure their messages are heartfelt and resonant? What role do virtual gestures, such as sending digital gifts or sharing multimedia expressions of affection, play in enhancing emotional intimacy? The exploration of the digital landscape of emotional intimacy unveils the ways in which couples actively infuse technology into the emotional fabric of their relationship.

Virtual Celebrations and Shared Moments:

Technology becomes a catalyst for virtual celebrations and shared moments, allowing couples to mark milestones, engage in shared activities, and create memories despite the physical distance. The role of technology in virtual celebrations prompts exploration into the ways in which couples plan and execute digital commemorations, the impact of shared virtual experiences on the relationship, and the creative use of technology to make special moments memorable.

How do couples utilize digital platforms to celebrate milestones and create shared experiences that contribute to the narrative of their relationship? What role does technology play in infusing joy and creativity into virtual celebrations, and how do partners navigate the challenges of making special moments memorable from afar? The exploration of virtual celebrations and shared moments unveils the ways in which couples actively integrate technology into the fabric of their relationship, turning distance into an opportunity for inventive and meaningful commemorations.

Creating Shared Digital Spaces:

Long-distance couples often seek to create shared digital spaces that serve as a surrogate for physical togetherness. From collaborative online journals to shared playlists and virtual games, these digital spaces become realms where partners can interact, share, and connect. The role of creating shared digital spaces prompts exploration into the ways in which couples craft a sense of belonging and shared identity in the virtual realm, the impact of these spaces on relationship dynamics, and the creative use of technology to foster togetherness.

How do partners engage in the creation of shared digital spaces, and what activities do they participate in to create a sense of shared presence? What impact do these digital spaces have on the emotional connection between partners, and how do they contribute to the overall vibrancy of the relationship? The exploration of creating shared digital spaces unveils the ways in which couples actively participate in the construction of a digital environment that mirrors the intimacy of physical togetherness.

Technology as a Bridge Across Time Zones:

The geographical dispersion in long-distance relationships often comes with significant time zone disparities, posing a challenge to coordination and communication. However, technology serves as a vital bridge across time zones, enabling partners to navigate the challenges of asynchronous communication, coordinate schedules, and maintain a sense of connection. The role of technology as a bridge across time zones prompts exploration into the ways in which couples leverage digital tools to overcome the temporal gap, the impact of technology on the frequency and quality of communication, and the strategies partners employ to synchronize their virtual presence.

How do couples use technology to navigate the challenges of time zone disparities, and what creative solutions do they employ to coordinate schedules? What impact does digital communication have on the emotional connection between partners when faced with significant time zone differences? The exploration of technology as a bridge across time zones unveils the ways in which couples actively engage in intentional communication to overcome the constraints of temporal separation.

Technology's Role in Overcoming Challenges:

Long-distance relationships are not without their challenges, and technology emerges as a powerful tool for overcoming these obstacles. The role of technology in overcoming challenges prompts exploration into the ways in which couples use digital platforms to address issues related to trust, communication, and emotional distance, the impact of technology on conflict resolution, and the strategies partners employ to navigate the complexities of a long-distance relationship.

How do couples actively use technology to address challenges related to trust and insecurity, and what role does digital communication play in resolving conflicts? What strategies do partners employ to maintain emotional closeness and navigate the complexities of emotional distance through digital means? The exploration of technology's role in overcoming challenges unveils the ways in which couples leverage digital tools as active agents in the resolution and mitigation of issues that arise in the unique context of long-distance love.

Innovation and Adaptability in the Digital Age:

The digital age fosters innovation and adaptability in long-distance relationships, with couples actively seeking out new technologies and platforms to enhance their connection. The role of innovation and adaptability in the digital age prompts exploration into the ways in which couples embrace emerging technologies, the impact of technological innovation on relationship dynamics, and the continuous process of adapting to new digital tools to sustain and enrich long-distance love.

How do couples stay abreast of emerging technologies, and what criteria do they use to incorporate new tools into their relationship? What impact does innovation have on the overall adaptability and resilience of long-distance relationships in the digital age? The exploration of innovation and adaptability in the digital age unveils the ways in which couples actively engage with the evolving landscape of technology to shape the contours of their modern love story.

In the realm of long-distance relationships, technology emerges not only as a facilitator of communication but as a transformative force that shapes the very essence of modern love. From virtual presence and shared experiences to overcoming challenges and fostering emotional intimacy, technology becomes an integral part of the narrative for couples navigating love across miles. Join us as we continue our exploration of virtual celebrations and long-distance love, delving into the diverse ways in which couples navigate the complexities and joys of modern romance.

Chapter 5: The Psychology of Love Today
Modern Psychosocial Perspectives on Love

Love, a complex and multifaceted emotion, undergoes continuous evolution influenced by societal changes, technological advancements, and shifting cultural norms. This chapter delves into the intricate world of modern psychosocial perspectives on love, exploring the psychological dynamics that shape contemporary romantic relationships.

Embracing Complexity:

In the modern landscape of love, psychologists and relationship experts emphasize the importance of embracing the complexity inherent in romantic relationships. Unlike traditional views that often sought simplicity in understanding love, contemporary perspectives acknowledge that love is a nuanced interplay of emotions, cognition, and behavior. Psychosocial perspectives encourage individuals and couples to navigate the intricacies of love with curiosity and an openness to the various dimensions that contribute to its richness.

How do modern psychosocial perspectives challenge traditional notions of simplicity in understanding love? What role does embracing complexity play in fostering resilience and adaptability within romantic relationships? The exploration of embracing complexity in love delves into the ways in which contemporary psychology encourages individuals to engage with the multifaceted nature of romantic connections.

Intersectionality and Love:

The recognition of intersectionality in contemporary psychology brings forth a crucial lens through which to understand love. Intersectionality acknowledges that individuals' experiences of love are deeply intertwined with other aspects of their identity, such as race, gender, sexual orientation, and socioeconomic status. Modern psychosocial perspectives on love explore how intersectionality influences relationship dynamics, personal narratives, and societal expectations.

How does intersectionality shape the experience of love for individuals with diverse backgrounds and identities? What impact does acknowledging the intersectionality of love have on dismantling stereotypes and fostering inclusivity within the realm of romantic relationships? The exploration of intersectionality and love unveils the ways in which contemporary psychology seeks to create a more inclusive and holistic understanding of romantic connections.

Attachment Theory in Modern Relationships:

Attachment theory, a cornerstone in understanding human relationships, undergoes nuanced examination in the context of modern love. Psychologists explore how attachment styles influence the dynamics of contemporary romantic relationships, examining the impact of secure, anxious, and avoidant attachments on communication, intimacy, and overall relationship satisfaction.

How does attachment theory contribute to the understanding of emotional bonds in modern romantic relationships? What challenges and opportunities do different attachment styles present in the context of evolving societal norms and expectations? The exploration of attachment theory in modern relationships unveils the ways in which psychologists adapt this framework to shed light on the intricacies of love in the 21st century.

Impact of Social Media on Relationship Satisfaction:

In the digital age, social media emerges as a significant factor influencing the psychology of love. Psychosocial perspectives delve into the impact of social media on relationship satisfaction, exploring how online platforms shape self-perception, communication styles, and the overall quality of romantic connections. The examination of social media's influence encompasses both positive and negative aspects, acknowledging the potential for connection and the challenges posed by comparison, jealousy, and digital communication nuances.

How does social media contribute to the construction of romantic narratives and self-identity within relationships? What role does online communication play in shaping the emotional landscape of love, and how do couples navigate the pitfalls associated with social media use? The exploration of the impact of social media on relationship satisfaction unveils the ways in which modern psychology grapples with the evolving digital dynamics of romantic connections.

Online Dating and the Psychology of Choice:

The advent of online dating transforms the psychology of partner selection and relationship initiation. Psychosocial perspectives on love today delve into the nuances of online dating, examining the impact of a vast array of choices, algorithmic matching, and the paradox of choice on individuals seeking romantic connections in the digital realm. The exploration of online dating's influence on the psychology of choice sheds light on decision-making processes, expectations, and the evolution of relationship preferences.

How does the abundance of choices in online dating platforms influence the psychology of partner selection? What role do algorithms play in shaping individuals' perceptions of compatibility and desirability in potential partners? The examination of online dating and the psychology of choice reveals the ways in which contemporary psychology grapples with the implications of technology on the initial stages of romantic relationships.

Digital Communication and Emotional Intimacy:

The role of digital communication in modern romantic relationships extends beyond convenience to impact the very fabric of emotional intimacy. Psychosocial perspectives explore how text messages, emojis, and virtual interactions contribute to the emotional landscape of love. The exploration of digital communication and emotional intimacy delves into the ways in which couples navigate the challenges and opportunities posed by technology in fostering a deep, meaningful connection.

How do couples use digital communication to express emotions and maintain a sense of closeness? What impact does the virtual dimension have on the perception of emotional cues, and how do partners adapt to the nuances of online communication? The examination of digital communication and emotional intimacy unveils the ways in which modern psychology grapples with the evolving language of love in the digital age.

Impact of Self-Perception in Social Media Relationships:

The visibility of romantic relationships on social media platforms introduces a layer of self-perception that can significantly influence individuals' experiences of love. Psychosocial perspectives explore how curated online representations of relationships shape self-esteem, validation, and the comparison game. The exploration of self-perception in social media relationships delves into the psychological effects of presenting and consuming idealized images of romantic connections.

How does the portrayal of relationships on social media impact individuals' self-esteem and self-worth? What role does comparison play in shaping perceptions of one's own relationship in the context of curated online content? The examination of self-perception in social media relationships unveils the ways in which modern psychology grapples with the interplay between digital presentation and individual well-being within romantic connections.

Psychology of Online Dating Profiles:

The construction of online dating profiles becomes a fascinating area of study within modern psychosocial perspectives on love. Psychologists explore how individuals curate and present aspects of their identity on dating platforms, examining the role of self-disclosure, authenticity, and the influence of societal expectations on profile creation. The exploration of the psychology of online dating profiles sheds light on the intricate dance between self-presentation and the pursuit of meaningful connections.

How do individuals navigate the balance between authenticity and self-promotion in online dating profiles? What impact does societal pressure and cultural expectations have on the construction of profiles seeking romantic connections? The examination of the psychology of online dating profiles unveils the ways in which modern psychology grapples with the intricacies of identity presentation in the pursuit of love in the digital realm.

The Role of Therapy in Navigating Modern Love:

As love becomes increasingly complex and diverse, the role of therapy in supporting individuals and couples takes center stage. Psychosocial perspectives explore how therapeutic interventions adapt to the unique challenges presented by modern romantic relationships. The exploration of the role of therapy in navigating modern love delves into the ways in which psychologists address issues such as communication breakdowns, digital communication challenges, and the evolving dynamics of partnership in the 21st century.

How do therapists incorporate psychosocial perspectives to address the challenges unique to modern love? What role does therapy play in helping individuals and couples navigate the impact of technology, societal expectations, and evolving relationship norms on their mental well-being? The examination of the role of therapy in navigating modern love unveils the ways in which psychology actively engages with the evolving landscape of romance to provide support and guidance.

In the intricate tapestry of modern psychosocial perspectives on love, psychologists, researchers, and relationship experts navigate the complexities of evolving societal norms, technological advancements, and the diverse expressions of romance. Join us as we continue our exploration of the psychology of love today, delving into the ways in which contemporary perspectives contribute to a deeper understanding of the intricate dance that is modern romance.

Impact of Social Media on Self-Perception in Relationships

In the era of interconnectedness and constant digital presence, the influence of social media on self-perception within romantic relationships has become a significant focal point for psychologists and relationship experts. This section delves into the intricate ways in which social media platforms shape individuals' perceptions of self within the context of their romantic connections.

The Curated Self on Display:

Social media platforms offer individuals a digital canvas on which they can curate and present aspects of their lives, including their romantic relationships. The curated self on display prompts exploration into how individuals navigate the delicate balance between authenticity and showcasing an idealized version of their love life. Psychologists examine the motivations behind curating the self on social media, the impact of external validation, and the nuances of self-expression within the realm of romantic connections.

How do individuals decide what aspects of their relationships to share on social media, and what drives the impulse to curate a curated self? What role does external validation play in shaping individuals' choices in presenting their romantic connections online? The exploration of the curated self on display unveils the complex interplay between self-expression, societal expectations, and the desire for affirmation within the context of modern love.

Comparison and the Perils of Social Media:

While social media offers a platform for connection and sharing, it also introduces the perils of comparison that can significantly impact individuals' self-perception within relationships. Psychologists delve into the psychological effects of comparing one's own romantic journey with the curated narratives of others on social media. The exploration of comparison and the perils of social media sheds light on the challenges individuals face in maintaining a healthy self-perception in the face of carefully crafted online representations.

How does the culture of comparison on social media influence individuals' perceptions of their own relationships and romantic achievements? What strategies can individuals employ to mitigate the negative impact of comparison on their self-esteem within the context of love? The examination of comparison and the perils of social media unveils the ways in which modern psychology grapples with the psychological challenges posed by the digital age.

Validation and the Quest for Likes:

The quest for validation through likes, comments, and shares on social media platforms becomes a psychological phenomenon that deeply intertwines with individuals' self-perception in relationships. Psychologists explore the motivations behind seeking validation online, the impact of digital affirmation on self-worth, and the potential consequences of tying one's worth to the metrics of social media engagement.

How does the pursuit of validation on social media intersect with individuals' self-esteem within the context of romantic relationships? What role does the dopamine-driven reward system of social media play in shaping the desire for digital affirmation? The exploration of validation and the quest for likes unveils the ways in which contemporary psychology navigates the complex terrain of seeking approval within the digital realm of modern love.

The Illusion of Perfection and Relationship Satisfaction:

Social media often presents an illusion of perfection, showcasing carefully selected moments that may not reflect the full spectrum of the romantic experience. Psychologists delve into how this illusion impacts individuals' perceptions of their own relationships and the potential consequences for overall relationship satisfaction. The examination of the illusion of perfection and relationship satisfaction explores the delicate balance between portraying positive aspects of love and creating unrealistic expectations.

How does the curated nature of social media content contribute to the illusion of perfection within romantic relationships? What impact does the perception of others' seemingly flawless love lives have on individuals' satisfaction with their own relationships? The exploration of the illusion of perfection and relationship satisfaction unveils the ways in which contemporary psychology grapples with the psychological consequences of consuming idealized representations of love.

Managing Expectations and Reality:

Navigating the juxtaposition of online representations with the reality of day-to-day relationships requires a nuanced understanding of self-perception. Psychologists explore how individuals manage their expectations based on social media narratives, examining the psychological strategies employed to bridge the gap between the digital fantasy and the tangible reality of romantic connections. The exploration of managing expectations and reality sheds light on the adaptive processes individuals employ to maintain a grounded self-perception within the complex landscape of modern love.

How do individuals distinguish between the idealized representations on social media and the authentic, sometimes imperfect, reality of their romantic relationships? What psychological strategies can individuals use to manage expectations and foster a healthy self-perception that aligns with the nuances of love? The examination of managing expectations and reality unveils the ways in which contemporary psychology grapples with the intricacies of maintaining mental well-being within the digital age of romantic connections.

Building Resilience Against Social Media Pressures:

The pressures exerted by social media on self-perception within relationships necessitate the cultivation of resilience. Psychologists explore the psychological tools individuals can develop to resist the negative impact of social media and build a robust sense of self within their romantic connections. The exploration of building resilience against social media pressures delves into the strategies that empower individuals to navigate the challenges posed by the digital realm without compromising their mental well-being.

What psychological factors contribute to an individual's resilience in the face of social media pressures related to love and relationships? How can individuals cultivate a healthy relationship with social media while safeguarding their self-perception and mental health? The examination of building resilience against social media pressures unveils the ways in which contemporary psychology actively engages with the task of empowering individuals to thrive in the digital landscape of modern love.

Fostering Authentic Connection in the Digital Age:

As social media continues to play a prominent role in shaping perceptions of self within relationships, psychologists explore avenues for fostering authentic connections in the digital age. The exploration of fostering authentic connection delves into the ways in which individuals and couples can leverage social media to enhance genuine expressions of love and intimacy while maintaining a healthy self-perception.

How can individuals balance the curated self on social media with authentic expressions of love within their relationships? What role do open communication, trust, and vulnerability play in fostering a sense of authenticity in the digital age of romantic connections? The examination of fostering authentic connection unveils the ways in which contemporary psychology actively contributes to the ongoing dialogue about maintaining genuine connections within the complex landscape of modern love.

In the ever-evolving landscape of love shaped by the digital age, the impact of social media on self-perception within relationships stands as a critical area of exploration for psychologists and individuals navigating the complexities of modern romance. Join us as we continue our journey into the psychology of love today, delving into the intricate ways in which contemporary perspectives contribute to a deeper understanding of self within the context of modern romantic connections.

Digital Communication and Emotional Intimacy

In the age of technology, the landscape of romantic relationships has been transformed by the advent of digital communication. This section explores the intricate interplay between digital communication and emotional intimacy, unraveling the ways in which technology shapes the emotional dynamics of modern love.

The Evolution of Digital Communication:

Digital communication has become an integral part of modern romance, reshaping how couples connect and share their emotional worlds. From the early days of email to the instantaneity of text messaging and the richness of video calls, the evolution of digital communication prompts exploration into the ways in which these technologies influence the expression and reception of emotions within romantic relationships.

How has the evolution of digital communication platforms impacted the emotional landscape of modern love? What role do different forms of digital communication play in shaping the depth and immediacy of emotional expression between partners? The exploration of the evolution of digital communication unveils the ways in which technology has become a conduit for emotional connection in the contemporary realm of romantic relationships.

Texting and the Nuances of Emotional Expression:

Text messaging stands as one of the primary modes of digital communication in romantic relationships, offering couples a constant channel for staying connected throughout the day. The nuances of emotional expression through texting prompt exploration into how individuals navigate the challenges and opportunities of conveying emotions through written words, emojis, and other digital symbols.

How do couples utilize text messaging to express a range of emotions, from joy and affection to frustration and vulnerability? What challenges arise in conveying emotional nuances through text, and how do couples overcome these obstacles? The exploration of texting and the nuances of emotional expression unveils the ways in which modern love adapts to the unique features of digital communication.

Emojis, GIFs, and Visual Emotional Cues:

In the realm of digital communication, emojis and GIFs have emerged as powerful tools for adding visual and emotional layers to textual interactions. The role of emojis, GIFs, and visual emotional cues prompts exploration into how couples use these digital symbols to enhance the expressiveness of their conversations and convey a spectrum of feelings.

How do couples incorporate emojis and GIFs into their digital communication to convey emotions that may be challenging to express with words alone? What impact do visual emotional cues have on the perception of tone and sentiment in digital interactions? The exploration of emojis, GIFs, and visual emotional cues unveils the ways in which couples creatively use these elements to enrich the emotional tapestry of their digital conversations.

Video Calls and Real-Time Emotional Connection:

Video calls have become a transformative element in digital communication, offering couples the opportunity for real-time, face-to-face interactions despite physical distances. The role of video calls in fostering real-time emotional connection prompts exploration into the ways in which couples leverage this technology to bridge the gap between them, share intimate moments, and sustain a sense of presence.

How do couples utilize video calls to create a sense of shared presence and enhance emotional intimacy? What impact does the visual dimension of video calls have on the depth of emotional connection between partners? The exploration of video calls and real-time emotional connection unveils the ways in which technology becomes a conduit for maintaining a profound and immediate bond in the digital age of romantic relationships.

Digital Communication and Misinterpretation:

While digital communication offers a multitude of expressive possibilities, it also introduces the potential for misinterpretation and misunderstandings. The dynamics of misinterpretation in digital communication prompt exploration into the challenges couples face in accurately decoding emotions, navigating the absence of non-verbal cues, and resolving conflicts that may arise from misaligned interpretations.

How do couples manage the risk of misinterpretation in digital communication, and what strategies can be employed to enhance clarity and understanding? What impact does misinterpretation have on emotional dynamics within romantic relationships, and how do couples work through challenges that arise from digital communication breakdowns? The exploration of digital communication and misinterpretation unveils the ways in which couples actively engage in the navigation of potential pitfalls in the digital landscape of love.

Digital Communication and Emotional Availability:

The constant connectivity facilitated by digital communication brings forth questions about emotional availability in the modern realm of romantic relationships. The exploration of digital communication and emotional availability delves into how individuals balance the benefits of staying connected throughout the day with the importance of creating intentional spaces for emotional availability and presence.

How does the constant stream of digital communication impact individuals' ability to be emotionally available to their partners? What role do intentional breaks from digital communication play in fostering emotional connection and presence within romantic relationships? The exploration of digital communication and emotional availability unveils the ways in which couples actively negotiate the boundaries of connectivity to maintain a healthy balance in the digital age of modern love.

Challenges and Opportunities in Digital Conflict Resolution:

Digital communication not only facilitates emotional expression but also becomes a battleground for conflict resolution within romantic relationships. The challenges and opportunities in digital conflict resolution prompt exploration into the ways in which couples navigate disagreements through text, email, or video calls, examining the unique dynamics of resolving conflicts in the digital realm.

How do couples approach conflict resolution in the digital age, and what strategies can be employed to address disagreements through digital communication? What challenges arise in resolving conflicts through text or other digital platforms, and how do couples overcome these obstacles to strengthen their emotional bond? The exploration of challenges and opportunities in digital conflict resolution unveils the ways in which modern love adapts to the unique landscape of resolving disputes in the digital realm.

Privacy, Trust, and Digital Communication:

The constant connectivity facilitated by digital communication brings forth questions about privacy and trust within romantic relationships. The exploration of privacy, trust, and digital communication delves into the ways in which couples negotiate the boundaries of personal space in the digital realm, building a foundation of trust that allows for open communication while respecting individual autonomy.

How do couples navigate the balance between staying connected digitally and respecting each other's need for privacy? What role does trust play in fostering open communication through digital platforms, and how is it maintained in the face of potential challenges? The exploration of privacy, trust, and digital communication unveils the ways in which modern love actively engages with issues of autonomy and connection in the digital age.

Digital Communication and Emotional Intimacy Across Distances:

For couples in long-distance relationships, digital communication becomes a lifeline, enabling them to maintain emotional intimacy despite physical separation. The exploration of digital communication and emotional intimacy across distances delves into the ways in which couples use technology to bridge the gap, share daily experiences, and create a sense of togetherness that transcends geographical boundaries.

How do couples in long-distance relationships utilize digital communication to create a shared emotional space and maintain a sense of closeness? What challenges and joys arise in fostering emotional intimacy across distances through technology, and how do couples navigate these dynamics? The exploration of digital communication and emotional intimacy across distances unveils the ways in which technology becomes a powerful tool for sustaining love in the face of geographical separation.

The Future of Digital Communication in Love:

As technology continues to advance, the future of digital communication in love holds promise for further innovations and transformations. The exploration of the future of digital communication in love delves into emerging technologies, potential shifts in communication patterns, and the ways in which couples may adapt to new tools that enhance the emotional dynamics of their relationships.

What emerging technologies are on the horizon that may reshape the landscape of digital communication in romantic relationships? How might future developments in virtual reality, augmented reality, or artificial intelligence impact the emotional intimacy between partners? The exploration of the future of digital communication in love unveils the ways in which modern love actively anticipates and engages with the ever-evolving landscape of technology.

In the intricate dance of modern love, digital communication emerges as a central player, influencing the depth, immediacy, and nuances of emotional intimacy between partners. Join us as we continue our exploration of the psychology of love today, delving into the ways in which contemporary perspectives contribute to a deeper understanding of the intricate interplay between technology and emotional connection in the digital age of romantic relationships.

Online Dating and its Psychological Effects

In the landscape of modern romance, online dating has emerged as a transformative force, reshaping the dynamics of how individuals meet, connect, and form romantic relationships. This section explores the psychological effects of online dating, delving into the intricate ways in which digital platforms influence the psychology of love.

The Rise of Online Dating:

The advent of the internet has revolutionized the way people seek romantic connections, giving rise to the phenomenon of online dating. The rise of online dating prompts exploration into the factors that have contributed to its popularity, from the convenience of digital platforms to the expanding pool of potential partners accessible through a few clicks.

How has online dating evolved over the years, and what cultural shifts have contributed to its widespread acceptance? What role do technological advancements play in the proliferation of online dating platforms, and how have they shaped the way individuals approach finding love in the digital age? The exploration of the rise of online dating unveils the ways in which technology has become a powerful mediator in the realm of modern romance.

Psychological Drivers of Online Dating:

The decision to engage in online dating is often influenced by a myriad of psychological factors, from the desire for companionship and connection to the quest for compatibility and shared values. The psychological drivers of online dating prompt exploration into the motivations that lead individuals to turn to digital platforms in their pursuit of love.

What psychological needs do online dating platforms fulfill, and how do they align with individuals' aspirations for romantic connections? How do factors such as personality traits, attachment styles, and life experiences influence the decision to explore online dating as a viable avenue for finding a partner? The exploration of the psychological drivers of online dating unveils the intricate interplay between individual motivations and the digital landscape of romantic exploration.

The Paradox of Choice and Decision-Making:

One of the unique challenges posed by online dating is the paradox of choice — the abundance of potential partners that can lead to decision fatigue and heightened expectations. The exploration of the paradox of choice and decision-making delves into how individuals navigate the vast array of profiles, make decisions about potential matches, and manage the psychological impact of seemingly limitless options.

How does the paradox of choice influence individuals' decision-making processes in online dating? What psychological effects can arise from having numerous options, and how do individuals cope with decision fatigue and the fear of missing out? The examination of the paradox of choice and decision-making unveils the ways in which online dating introduces unique challenges to the psychological landscape of romantic exploration.

Constructing Online Identities:

Online dating necessitates the construction of digital identities that represent individuals in the digital realm. The exploration of constructing online identities delves into the ways in which individuals curate and present aspects of their personality, interests, and lifestyle on dating profiles, examining the psychological motivations behind self-presentation and the potential impact on the perception of authenticity.

How do individuals navigate the delicate balance between authenticity and self-promotion when constructing online identities? What role do societal expectations, cultural norms, and personal values play in shaping the way individuals present themselves on dating platforms? The exploration of constructing online identities unveils the complex interplay between self-perception, societal influences, and the pursuit of meaningful connections in the digital age.

The Role of Algorithms and Compatibility Matching:

Online dating platforms often employ algorithms and compatibility matching systems to streamline the matchmaking process. The role of algorithms and compatibility matching prompts exploration into how these technological tools influence individuals' perceptions of compatibility, partner selection, and the overall success of online dating experiences.

How do individuals perceive the reliability and effectiveness of algorithms in predicting compatibility and facilitating meaningful connections? What impact does the use of algorithms have on the dynamics of online dating, and how do individuals balance algorithmic recommendations with their own intuition and preferences? The exploration of the role of algorithms and compatibility matching unveils the ways in which technology shapes the decision-making processes in the pursuit of love.

Online Dating and the Experience of Rejection:

The nature of online dating introduces the possibility of rejection, whether through the initial swiping process or after engaging in conversations. The experience of rejection in online dating prompts exploration into the psychological effects it may have on individuals, examining coping mechanisms, self-esteem implications, and the potential influence on future romantic pursuits.

How do individuals cope with the experience of rejection in the context of online dating? What role does rejection play in shaping self-perception and resilience within the digital landscape of romantic exploration? The examination of online dating and the experience of rejection unveils the ways in which individuals navigate the emotional challenges inherent in the pursuit of love through digital platforms.

Online Dating and the Formation of Intimacy:

Despite the potential challenges, online dating has also been successful in facilitating the formation of intimate connections and long-term relationships. The exploration of online dating and the formation of intimacy delves into how individuals navigate the stages of digital courtship, from initial online interactions to the transition into offline relationships, examining the psychological factors that contribute to the development of emotional closeness.

How do individuals foster emotional intimacy through online communication, and what role does digital interaction play in the formation of deep, meaningful connections? What challenges and joys arise in transitioning from online to offline interactions, and how do individuals navigate this crucial phase of romantic exploration? The exploration of online dating and the formation of intimacy unveils the ways in which digital platforms can become catalysts for profound emotional connections.

Challenges and Ethical Considerations in Online Dating:

Online dating is not without its challenges and ethical considerations. The exploration of challenges and ethical considerations in online dating delves into issues such as catfishing, deceptive practices, and the potential for harm in the digital dating landscape, examining how these challenges impact individuals' mental well-being and the overall trustworthiness of online platforms.

How do individuals protect themselves from deceptive practices and potential harm in the world of online dating? What role do ethical considerations play in shaping individuals' choices and behaviors within digital dating spaces? The examination of challenges and ethical considerations in online dating unveils the ways in which individuals and the online dating industry grapple with the responsibility of creating safe and authentic spaces for romantic exploration.

Long-Term Effects of Online Dating on Relationship Satisfaction:

As online dating becomes a common avenue for finding love, questions arise about its long-term effects on relationship satisfaction. The exploration of long-term effects of online dating on relationship satisfaction delves into research findings, psychological studies, and real-life narratives to understand how the initial digital encounters translate into lasting, fulfilling relationships.

What insights do studies provide regarding the long-term success and satisfaction of relationships that began through online dating? How do individuals who found love online navigate the challenges and joys of building a life together, and what factors contribute to the durability of these relationships? The exploration of long-term effects of online dating on relationship satisfaction unveils the ways in which technology continues to shape the trajectory of modern love.

Balancing Digital and Offline Romance:

In the pursuit of love, individuals often find themselves balancing the digital and offline realms of romance. The exploration of balancing digital and offline romance delves into the ways in which individuals navigate the integration of online dating into their broader romantic journeys, examining how technology serves as a complement to, rather than a replacement for, traditional forms of romantic exploration.

How do individuals strike a balance between the convenience of online dating and the richness of face-to-face interactions? What role does intentional offline engagement play in building authentic connections, and how do individuals maintain a holistic approach to romantic exploration in the digital age? The exploration of balancing digital and offline romance unveils the ways in which individuals actively shape the narrative of their romantic lives, leveraging technology as a tool within the broader landscape of modern love.

The Evolution of Online Dating Culture:

As online dating culture continues to evolve, so do societal attitudes, norms, and expectations surrounding digital romance. The exploration of the evolution of online dating culture delves into shifts in public perception, the impact of technology on societal views of love, and the ways in which online dating has become an integral part of the broader cultural landscape.

How has the cultural perception of online dating shifted over time, and what role does it currently play in shaping societal views of love and relationships? How do individuals and communities engage with and adapt to the evolving landscape of online dating culture? The exploration of the evolution of online dating culture unveils the ways in which technology intersects with societal norms to redefine the narrative of modern romance.

In the dynamic landscape of modern love, online dating stands as a powerful force, influencing the way individuals navigate the complex terrain of romantic exploration. Join us as we continue our exploration of the psychology of love today, delving into the ways in which contemporary perspectives contribute to a deeper understanding of the intricate interplay between technology and the pursuit of meaningful connections in the digital age of romantic relationships.

Chapter 6: Love in the Age of Globalization
Cross-Cultural Relationships and International Love

In the era of globalization, the world has become more interconnected than ever, leading to a rise in cross-cultural relationships and international love. This section explores the nuances, challenges, and joys of love that transcends geographical and cultural boundaries, delving into the psychological and emotional dynamics that shape these unique connections.

The Tapestry of Cross-Cultural Love:

Cross-cultural relationships weave a rich tapestry of diversity, encompassing connections between individuals from different countries, ethnicities, and cultural backgrounds. The exploration of the tapestry of cross-cultural love delves into the ways in which these relationships navigate the complexities of blending diverse traditions, values, and perspectives to create a harmonious and meaningful connection.

How do individuals in cross-cultural relationships negotiate and celebrate the diversity within their partnership? What role do open communication, curiosity, and mutual respect play in fostering a deep understanding and appreciation of each other's cultural backgrounds? The examination of the tapestry of cross-cultural love unveils the ways in which these relationships contribute to the evolving narrative of modern love.

The Allure of International Love:

International love holds a unique allure, drawing individuals to seek romantic connections beyond the borders of their own countries. The exploration of the allure of international love delves into the factors that contribute to the appeal of cross-cultural relationships, from the excitement of discovering new perspectives to the potential for personal growth and enrichment.

What motivates individuals to pursue international love, and how do these motivations shape the dynamics of cross-cultural relationships? How does the allure of international love contribute to the broader landscape of modern romance, challenging traditional notions of geographical constraints in matters of the heart? The examination of the allure of international love unveils the ways in which global connectivity reshapes the possibilities and aspirations of romantic connections.

Navigating Cultural Differences:

While cross-cultural relationships offer a unique and enriching experience, they also come with the challenge of navigating cultural differences. The exploration of navigating cultural differences delves into how individuals in cross-cultural relationships navigate potential misunderstandings, differing communication styles, and varying expectations rooted in cultural norms.

How do couples in cross-cultural relationships address and embrace the differences in their cultural backgrounds? What role does open dialogue, cultural sensitivity, and adaptability play in overcoming challenges and fostering a harmonious connection? The examination of navigating cultural differences unveils the ways in which love transcends cultural boundaries, encouraging individuals to bridge the gaps and create a shared understanding.

Language as a Bridge and Barrier:

In cross-cultural relationships, language becomes a crucial element that can both bridge and be a barrier to understanding. The exploration of language as a bridge and barrier delves into how couples navigate linguistic challenges, the role of multilingualism in fostering connection, and the potential for miscommunication that arises when partners speak different native languages.

How do individuals in cross-cultural relationships use language as a tool for connection, expression, and intimacy? What challenges and joys arise when partners speak different native languages, and how do couples overcome language barriers to build a strong and resilient connection? The examination of language as a bridge and barrier unveils the intricate ways in which communication shapes the dynamics of international love.

Celebrating Cultural Diversity in Relationships:

Cross-cultural relationships offer a unique opportunity to celebrate and incorporate the richness of cultural diversity into the fabric of love. The exploration of celebrating cultural diversity in relationships delves into the ways in which couples embrace and integrate each other's cultural traditions, customs, and celebrations, fostering an environment of inclusivity and shared experiences.

How do individuals in cross-cultural relationships create a space for the celebration of cultural diversity within their partnership? What role does cultural exchange, participation in each other's traditions, and the blending of cultural elements play in strengthening the bond between partners? The examination of celebrating cultural diversity in relationships unveils the ways in which love becomes a platform for the appreciation and celebration of global heritage.

Family Dynamics and Cross-Cultural Unions:

In cross-cultural relationships, the merging of families from different cultural backgrounds introduces another layer of complexity. The exploration of family dynamics and cross-cultural unions delves into the ways in which couples navigate the expectations, traditions, and values of extended families, examining the role of familial support or resistance in shaping the trajectory of these relationships.

How do couples in cross-cultural unions manage potential challenges related to familial expectations and cultural differences? What role does open communication and education play in fostering understanding and acceptance among family members from diverse cultural backgrounds? The examination of family dynamics and cross-cultural unions unveils the ways in which love becomes a bridge that connects not only individuals but also their families across cultural divides.

Transcending Geographical Distances in International Love:

International love often involves transcending not only cultural but also geographical distances. The exploration of transcending geographical distances in international love delves into the ways in which couples navigate the challenges and joys of long-distance relationships across borders, examining the role of technology, communication, and intentional efforts in sustaining connection despite physical separation.

How do individuals in international long-distance relationships maintain a sense of closeness and intimacy despite being separated by vast distances? What role does technology play in bridging the gap, and how do couples cultivate trust and emotional connection across time zones? The examination of transcending geographical distances in international love unveils the ways in which modern technology becomes a lifeline for couples seeking love across borders.

The Impact of Globalization on Relationship Expectations:

Globalization has not only facilitated the rise of cross-cultural relationships but has also influenced relationship expectations in the modern era. The exploration of the impact of globalization on relationship expectations delves into how individuals in cross-cultural unions navigate evolving norms, expectations, and aspirations influenced by the broader globalized culture.

How does globalization shape individuals' expectations regarding love, partnership, and the trajectory of their relationships? What role do societal shifts, media influence, and exposure to diverse cultural narratives play in shaping the expectations of individuals engaged in cross-cultural love? The examination of the impact of globalization on relationship expectations unveils the ways in which modern love becomes a dynamic force, adapting to and influencing the evolving landscape of globalized romance.

Challenges and Resilience in Cross-Cultural Love:

While cross-cultural love offers unique rewards, it also comes with its set of challenges. The exploration of challenges and resilience in cross-cultural love delves into the potential difficulties that individuals may encounter, from societal prejudices to personal insecurities, examining the ways in which couples build resilience, overcome obstacles, and emerge stronger in the face of adversity.

How do individuals in cross-cultural relationships navigate societal expectations and potential biases against their union? What strategies do couples employ to build resilience and maintain a strong connection when faced with challenges rooted in cultural differences? The examination of challenges and resilience in cross-cultural love unveils the ways in which love becomes a powerful force for growth and transformation in the context of globalized romance.

The Role of Travel in Cross-Cultural Love Stories:

In cross-cultural love stories, travel often plays a significant role, providing opportunities for individuals to explore each other's cultural contexts, connect with families, and create shared memories in diverse locations. The exploration of the role of travel in cross-cultural love stories delves into the ways in which couples use travel as a means of deepening their connection, fostering mutual understanding, and building a life enriched by a variety of cultural experiences.

How do couples in cross-cultural relationships incorporate travel into their love stories, and what impact does it have on their bond? What role does shared exploration of new environments play in creating lasting memories and strengthening the foundation of cross-cultural unions? The examination of the role of travel in cross-cultural love stories unveils the ways in which adventurous spirits and a shared love for exploration contribute to the narrative of modern love.

The Future of Cross-Cultural Relationships:

As the world continues to become more interconnected, the future of cross-cultural relationships holds promise for further growth, understanding, and acceptance. The exploration of the future of cross-cultural relationships delves into emerging trends, potential shifts in societal attitudes, and the ways in which global connectivity may continue to shape the dynamics of international love.

What emerging trends are on the horizon for cross-cultural relationships, and how might they influence the landscape of modern love? How can individuals and societies actively contribute to fostering a more inclusive and accepting environment for cross-cultural unions? The examination of the future of cross-cultural relationships unveils the ways in which love becomes a catalyst for building bridges across cultures and embracing the diversity that defines the globalized world.

In the vibrant tapestry of modern love, cross-cultural relationships and international love stand as testaments to the boundless nature of human connection. Join us as we continue our exploration of the psychology of love today, delving into the ways in which contemporary perspectives contribute to a deeper understanding of the intricate interplay between cultures, hearts, and the evolving narrative of love in the age of globalization.

Global Perspectives on Love and Marriage

In the ever-expanding landscape of globalization, love and marriage are undergoing transformations influenced by diverse cultural norms, societal expectations, and individual aspirations. This section explores global perspectives on love and marriage, delving into the ways in which different societies approach and navigate the complex tapestry of romantic relationships.

The Cultural Kaleidoscope of Love:

Love is a universal human experience, yet its expression and manifestation vary dramatically across cultures. The exploration of the cultural kaleidoscope of love delves into the diverse ways in which different societies conceptualize, express, and celebrate love. From arranged marriages to passionate romances, the kaleidoscope captures the myriad ways in which love is woven into the fabric of cultures around the world.

How do cultural traditions and values shape the expression of love within different societies? What role do familial expectations, societal norms, and religious beliefs play in influencing the trajectory of romantic relationships? The examination of the cultural kaleidoscope of love unveils the richness and complexity that emerges when love intertwines with the diverse tapestry of global cultures.

Arranged Marriages and Cultural Continuity:

Arranged marriages, a practice deeply rooted in various cultures, present a unique perspective on the intersection of love and cultural continuity. The exploration of arranged marriages and cultural continuity delves into how this age-old tradition persists in the modern era, examining the role of families, matchmakers, and societal expectations in shaping the union of individuals within the framework of cultural norms.

How do individuals in cultures with arranged marriages navigate the balance between personal agency and familial expectations? What role does the preservation of cultural heritage and social harmony play in the continuation of arranged marriage practices? The examination of arranged marriages and cultural continuity unveils the ways in which love becomes intertwined with familial and cultural considerations.

Love in the Modern Urban Landscape:

Urbanization and globalization have ushered in a new era, influencing the dynamics of love and marriage in modern urban settings. The exploration of love in the modern urban landscape delves into the ways in which individuals navigate the challenges and opportunities presented by cosmopolitan environments. From the impact of career aspirations to changing gender roles, love in urban settings reflects the evolving nature of societal structures.

How does the modern urban landscape shape individuals' attitudes toward love, marriage, and partnership? What role does the pursuit of individual goals and ambitions play in the decision-making processes of romantic relationships? The examination of love in the modern urban landscape unveils the intricate interplay between societal shifts, personal aspirations, and the pursuit of meaningful connections.

Love Beyond Borders: International Marriages:

The phenomenon of international marriages highlights the global interconnectedness of love, transcending national boundaries. The exploration of love beyond borders and international marriages delves into how individuals from different countries navigate the complexities of cross-cultural unions, examining the role of shared values, mutual understanding, and the blending of diverse traditions.

What motivates individuals to pursue international marriages, and how do they navigate the challenges of cultural differences and geographical distances? How does the globalized world contribute to the increasing prevalence and acceptance of international marriages? The examination of love beyond borders unveils the ways in which globalization transforms the landscape of romantic unions, fostering connections that transcend national borders.

Changing Dynamics of Gender Roles in Love and Marriage:

The evolving understanding of gender roles has profound implications for the dynamics of love and marriage worldwide. The exploration of changing dynamics of gender roles in love and marriage delves into how societies grapple with shifting expectations, empowerment of women, and the redefinition of traditional gender roles within romantic relationships.

How do changing gender dynamics influence the expectations and experiences of individuals in love and marriage? What role do societal attitudes, legal frameworks, and cultural norms play in shaping the evolving narrative of gender roles within romantic unions? The examination of changing dynamics of gender roles unveils the ways in which love becomes a transformative force, challenging and reshaping societal norms.

Love in the Face of Cultural Stigma:

In some cultures, love can be met with resistance or cultural stigma, especially when it defies established norms or expectations. The exploration of love in the face of cultural stigma delves into the challenges individuals may encounter when pursuing relationships that go against societal expectations. From interfaith relationships to unconventional partnerships, this exploration unveils the resilience and determination of individuals who navigate love despite cultural opposition.

How do individuals in relationships facing cultural stigma overcome societal barriers and biases? What role does personal conviction, resilience, and community support play in challenging cultural norms that may hinder the pursuit of unconventional love? The examination of love in the face of cultural stigma unveils the ways in which individuals forge paths that honor personal authenticity and connection.

Marriage as a Social Contract:

In some societies, marriage extends beyond the realm of personal connection and is viewed as a social contract with broader implications for families and communities. The exploration of marriage as a social contract delves into how cultural, economic, and familial considerations influence the decision-making processes around matrimony, examining the role of unions in preserving social structures and upholding societal norms.

How does the perception of marriage as a social contract shape individuals' choices and responsibilities within romantic unions? What impact does this perspective have on the stability and cohesion of families and communities? The examination of marriage as a social contract unveils the ways in which love becomes entwined with broader societal considerations.

Love in the Digital Age:

Globalization is closely intertwined with technological advancements, and the digital age has transformed the landscape of love and marriage. The exploration of love in the digital age delves into how technology facilitates and shapes romantic connections, from online dating platforms to virtual ceremonies, examining the ways in which the digital realm intersects with the pursuit of love on a global scale.

How does technology influence the initial stages of romantic connections in a globalized world? What role does digital communication play in sustaining long-distance relationships and fostering global connections? The examination of love in the digital age unveils the ways in which technology becomes a bridge, connecting individuals across geographical distances and cultural boundaries.

Love and Intercultural Communication:

Effective communication is fundamental to the success of any relationship, and intercultural communication becomes paramount in the context of cross-cultural love. The exploration of love and intercultural communication delves into the ways in which individuals in cross-cultural relationships navigate linguistic and cultural differences, examining the role of effective communication in building understanding and connection.

How do individuals in cross-cultural relationships develop skills in intercultural communication? What challenges and joys arise when partners communicate across language and cultural barriers, and how do they enhance their ability to connect authentically? The examination of love and intercultural communication unveils the ways in which effective communication becomes a cornerstone for the success of cross-cultural unions.

The Future of Love and Marriage in a Globalized World:

As the world continues to evolve through globalization, the future of love and marriage holds both challenges and possibilities. The exploration of the future of love and marriage in a globalized world delves into emerging trends, societal shifts, and the ways in which individuals and communities may shape the narrative of romantic relationships on a global scale.

What emerging trends are on the horizon for love and marriage in a globalized world, and how might they impact the dynamics of romantic unions? How can individuals actively contribute to fostering a more inclusive, understanding, and accepting environment for love to thrive in the era of globalization? The examination of the future of love and marriage unveils the ways in which modern romance continues to adapt, transform, and shape the interconnected world of globalized love.

In the diverse landscapes of love and marriage globally, myriad stories unfold, reflecting the intricacies and beauty of human connections. Join us as we continue our exploration of the psychology of love today, delving into the ways in which contemporary perspectives contribute to a deeper understanding of the intricate interplay between cultures, hearts, and the evolving narrative of love in the age of globalization.

Challenges and Advantages of Globalized Love

Love in a globalized world presents a tapestry woven with both challenges and advantages, reflecting the complex nature of romantic relationships in an interconnected and diverse society. This section explores the nuances of globalized love, shedding light on the obstacles faced and the unique benefits experienced by individuals navigating relationships across cultural and geographical boundaries.

Navigating Cross-Cultural Challenges:

One of the primary challenges of globalized love lies in navigating the intricate web of cross-cultural differences. When individuals from diverse cultural backgrounds come together, they often encounter disparities in traditions, values, and communication styles. The exploration of navigating cross-cultural challenges delves into the complexities faced by couples in cross-cultural relationships, examining how they negotiate and bridge the gaps between their respective cultural worlds.

How do individuals in globalized relationships address cultural misunderstandings and differences? What role does open communication, curiosity, and a willingness to learn play in overcoming cross-cultural challenges? The examination of navigating cross-cultural challenges unveils the ways in which love becomes a catalyst for growth, understanding, and the forging of connections that transcend cultural divides.

The Impact of Distance on Relationships:

Globalized love frequently involves relationships that span vast geographical distances. While technology has facilitated communication, the impact of physical separation remains a significant challenge. The exploration of the impact of distance on relationships delves into how couples navigate the emotional and practical challenges of being separated by oceans and time zones.

How do individuals in long-distance relationships maintain a sense of closeness and intimacy despite the physical distance? What role does technology play in bridging the gap, and how do couples cope with the challenges of time differences and limited face-to-face interactions? The examination of the impact of distance on relationships unveils the resilience and creativity of couples committed to making globalized love work.

Legal and Immigration Challenges:

Globalized love often involves individuals from different countries, introducing legal and immigration challenges that can impact the trajectory of relationships. The exploration of legal and immigration challenges delves into the complexities faced by couples navigating visa regulations, residency requirements, and the legal intricacies of international partnerships.

How do legal and immigration challenges influence the decisions and timelines of individuals in globalized relationships? What role does government policy play in shaping the possibilities for couples seeking to build a life together across borders? The examination of legal and immigration challenges unveils the ways in which external factors can shape the course of globalized love stories.

Time Zone and Communication Barriers:

In a globalized world, couples often find themselves dealing with time zone differences that can create communication challenges. The exploration of time zone and communication barriers delves into how couples overcome the logistical obstacles of coordinating schedules, ensuring meaningful communication, and staying connected despite the constraints imposed by different time zones.

How do individuals in globalized relationships navigate the practicalities of time zone differences to maintain regular and meaningful communication? What role does flexibility, understanding, and intentional efforts play in overcoming time-related challenges in relationships? The examination of time zone and communication barriers unveils the ways in which couples adapt to the realities of a world that operates across different clocks.

Cultural Sensitivity and Understanding:

Cultural sensitivity is paramount in globalized love, as individuals must navigate diverse perspectives, traditions, and social norms. The exploration of cultural sensitivity and understanding delves into how couples cultivate an awareness and appreciation of each other's cultural backgrounds, fostering an environment of mutual respect and acceptance.

How do individuals in globalized relationships develop cultural sensitivity, and what role does education and exposure play in shaping their understanding of different cultural contexts? What challenges arise when partners hold contrasting cultural values, and how do couples navigate potential conflicts with grace and empathy? The examination of cultural sensitivity and understanding unveils the ways in which love becomes a bridge that transcends cultural differences.

Balancing Individual Aspirations:

Globalized love often involves individuals with diverse personal aspirations, career goals, and life plans. The exploration of balancing individual aspirations delves into how couples navigate the complexities of pursuing personal goals while maintaining a harmonious and supportive partnership.

How do individuals in globalized relationships balance the pursuit of individual aspirations with the commitment to a shared life? What role does compromise, communication, and mutual support play in fostering a dynamic where both partners can thrive personally and within the relationship? The examination of balancing individual aspirations unveils the ways in which love becomes a source of encouragement and empowerment for individuals on unique and interconnected journeys.

Adapting to Changing Societal Norms:

Globalized love is often subject to evolving societal norms and expectations, which can impact the dynamics of relationships. The exploration of adapting to changing societal norms delves into how couples navigate the external pressures and influences that may shape their relationship, examining the role of resilience, communication, and a shared vision for the future.

How do individuals in globalized relationships respond to societal shifts in attitudes towards love, marriage, and cultural diversity? What challenges and advantages arise when couples find themselves at the intersection of evolving societal norms and their personal connection? The examination of adapting to changing societal norms unveils the ways in which love becomes a force that transcends external influences, allowing couples to define their own narrative.

Financial Considerations and Inequality:

Globalized love may also encounter financial considerations and inequalities, particularly when individuals come from different economic backgrounds or face disparities in earning potential. The exploration of financial considerations and inequality delves into how couples navigate discussions about money, address imbalances, and build a financial foundation that supports the aspirations and well-being of both partners.

How do individuals in globalized relationships approach financial discussions, and what role does transparency and shared financial planning play in building a stable partnership? What challenges arise when partners face economic disparities, and how do couples work towards creating a sense of financial equality? The examination of financial considerations and inequality unveils the ways in which love becomes a collaborative effort in navigating the complexities of economic dynamics.

Embracing Diversity in Parenting Styles:

For couples in globalized relationships who decide to build families, embracing diversity in parenting styles becomes a central consideration. The exploration of diversity in parenting styles delves into how couples navigate the challenges and advantages of merging different cultural approaches to parenting, examining the role of communication, compromise, and the creation of a parenting philosophy that reflects the shared values of the family.

How do individuals in globalized relationships negotiate the integration of diverse cultural parenting styles? What role does open dialogue play in addressing potential conflicts or differences in approaches to raising children? The examination of diversity in parenting styles unveils the ways in which love becomes a guiding force in the creation of a family culture that reflects the richness of diverse backgrounds.

Advantages of Globalized Love:

Amidst the challenges, globalized love also brings forth unique advantages that contribute to the richness and depth of relationships. The exploration of the advantages of globalized love delves into the positive aspects that arise from navigating diverse cultural landscapes, building connections that transcend borders, and embracing the opportunities presented by a globalized world.

How do individuals in globalized relationships benefit from exposure to different cultural perspectives, traditions, and ways of life? What advantages arise from the shared experience of overcoming challenges and building a connection that transcends geographical distances? The examination of the advantages of globalized love unveils the ways in which love becomes a transformative and enriching force, contributing to personal growth, expanded horizons, and a deepened understanding of the human experience.

Globalized Love as a Catalyst for Personal Growth:

One of the significant advantages of globalized love lies in its potential to serve as a catalyst for personal growth. The exploration of globalized love as a catalyst for personal growth delves into how individuals in international relationships experience personal development, self-discovery, and the expansion of their perspectives through the unique challenges and opportunities presented by a globalized connection.

How does navigating the complexities of globalized love contribute to individuals' self-awareness, adaptability, and resilience? What role does the exposure to different cultures, traditions, and ways of thinking play in shaping personal growth within the context of a globalized relationship? The examination of globalized love as a catalyst for personal growth unveils the ways in which love becomes a transformative journey of self-discovery and evolution.

Building a Global Support System:

Globalized love often extends beyond the immediate couple, creating opportunities to build a diverse and expansive support system. The exploration of building a global support system delves into how individuals in international relationships connect with communities, friends, and extended families across different parts of the world, creating a network that enhances the richness of their shared experiences.

How do individuals in globalized relationships foster connections with communities that span different cultural and geographical realms? What advantages arise from having a global support system that provides diverse perspectives, insights, and sources of encouragement? The examination of building a global support system unveils the ways in which love becomes a bridge that connects individuals not only to each other but also to a broader, interconnected world.

Contributing to Cultural Understanding and Harmony:

Globalized love has the potential to contribute to cultural understanding and harmony, fostering a world where diverse perspectives are embraced and celebrated. The exploration of contributing to cultural understanding and harmony delves into how individuals in globalized relationships become ambassadors of cross-cultural empathy, breaking down stereotypes, and promoting a deeper appreciation for the beauty of diversity.

How do couples in globalized relationships actively contribute to cultural understanding within their communities and beyond? What advantages arise from the role of love in transcending cultural divides and fostering a sense of unity in a globalized world? The examination of contributing to cultural understanding and harmony unveils the ways in which love becomes a powerful force for positive change, shaping attitudes and perceptions towards cultural diversity.

Globalized Love as a Source of Inspiration:

Globalized love serves as a source of inspiration, generating narratives that resonate with individuals around the world. The exploration of globalized love as a source of inspiration delves into how stories of cross-cultural connections, resilience, and shared experiences inspire others to embrace the possibilities of love in a globalized era.

How do narratives of globalized love contribute to a collective understanding of the human experience and the potential for deep, meaningful connections across borders? What role does storytelling play in sharing the diverse and inspiring tales of love that transcend cultural and geographical boundaries? The examination of globalized love as a source of inspiration unveils the ways in which love becomes a universal language that speaks to the shared aspirations, challenges, and triumphs of the human heart.

Conclusion: Embracing the Complexity of Globalized Love:

In the vibrant tapestry of globalized love, embracing the complexity becomes essential for individuals navigating the challenges and advantages of relationships that transcend borders. The exploration of globalized love is a journey that unfolds with each unique connection, contributing to the evolving narrative of modern romance in an interconnected world.

As we conclude our exploration of love in the age of globalization, we invite you to reflect on the stories, challenges, and advantages presented in this chapter. From the intricacies of cross-cultural love to the transformative power of globalized connections, love in a globalized world emerges as a dynamic and enriching force that transcends boundaries and shapes the narrative of contemporary romance.

Join us in the next chapter as we delve into the future trends of love and relationships, anticipating the ways in which the evolving landscape of technology, societal norms, and individual aspirations may influence the trajectory of modern love stories.

The Role of Travel in Modern Love Stories

In the intricate dance of modern love, travel emerges as a transformative and enriching companion, shaping the narratives of couples across borders and cultures. This section explores the multifaceted role of travel in modern love stories, delving into how the exploration of new landscapes, cultures, and experiences becomes an integral part of the tapestry of globalized relationships.

Shared Adventures and Creating Memories:

Travel serves as a canvas for shared adventures, allowing couples in globalized relationships to create memories that transcend the ordinary. Whether exploring vibrant cityscapes, traversing serene landscapes, or immersing themselves in cultural festivities, the shared experiences of travel become the building blocks of a unique and shared history.

How do couples in globalized relationships use travel to create lasting memories? What role do shared adventures play in deepening the bond and fostering a sense of unity? The exploration of shared adventures and creating memories unveils the ways in which travel becomes a vehicle for building a rich tapestry of experiences that defines the narrative of modern love.

Exploring Each Other's Cultural Contexts:

One of the distinctive aspects of globalized love is the opportunity to explore each other's cultural contexts through travel. Visiting hometowns, meeting extended families, and participating in cultural celebrations provide couples with insights into the diverse backgrounds that shape their identities.

How do individuals in globalized relationships navigate the exploration of each other's cultural contexts through travel? What impact does immersing oneself in the traditions and daily life of a partner's culture have on the dynamics of the relationship? The examination of exploring each other's cultural contexts unveils the ways in which travel becomes a bridge, fostering understanding and appreciation.

Connecting with Families Across Borders:

Travel facilitates the important connection with families across borders, allowing individuals in globalized relationships to forge meaningful bonds with their partner's relatives. Visiting family members, participating in familial traditions, and experiencing the warmth of familial connections contribute to the fabric of love that extends beyond the couple.

How do couples navigate the dynamics of meeting and connecting with each other's families across borders? What role does travel play in fostering a sense of belonging and acceptance within extended familial circles? The exploration of connecting with families across borders unveils the ways in which travel becomes a conduit for building bridges and expanding the sense of family in globalized love stories.

Romantic Retreats and Rejuvenation:

Travel offers couples in globalized relationships the opportunity for romantic retreats, providing a break from the routines of daily life and creating spaces for rejuvenation. Whether it's a secluded beach, a charming mountain retreat, or a bustling city escape, romantic getaways become a means of nurturing the romantic flame and deepening the emotional connection.

How do couples incorporate romantic retreats into their relationship dynamics, and what impact does this intentional focus on romance have on the overall health of the relationship? What role does travel play in providing moments of relaxation and reconnection in the midst of the challenges of globalized love? The examination of romantic retreats and rejuvenation unveils the ways in which travel becomes a source of nourishment for the heart and soul.

Navigating Cross-Cultural Celebrations:

Travel often involves navigating cross-cultural celebrations, from traditional festivals to familial milestones. The exploration of navigating cross-cultural celebrations delves into how couples in globalized relationships approach and participate in cultural festivities, incorporating diverse traditions into the tapestry of their shared experiences.

How do individuals in globalized relationships navigate the intricacies of cross-cultural celebrations, and what significance do these shared experiences hold for the relationship? What role does travel play in creating a space for cultural exchange and mutual celebration? The examination of navigating cross-cultural celebrations unveils the ways in which travel becomes a catalyst for the fusion of diverse traditions and the creation of new, shared rituals.

Adventure as a Bonding Experience:

The spirit of adventure becomes a bonding experience for couples in globalized relationships who embrace the thrill of exploring new places and trying new activities together. Whether it's embarking on a hiking expedition, diving into local cuisine, or navigating unfamiliar streets, the shared sense of adventure becomes a powerful glue that binds hearts.

How do couples in globalized relationships infuse a spirit of adventure into their travels, and what impact does this shared exploration have on the dynamics of the relationship?

What role does the element of surprise and novelty play in keeping the spark alive in globalized love stories? The exploration of adventure as a bonding experience unveils the ways in which travel becomes a dynamic and invigorating force in modern love.

Building a Global Home Together:

Travel contributes to the process of building a global home for couples in globalized relationships. Whether it involves exploring potential places to settle, envisioning a future together in different parts of the world, or creating a home that reflects the fusion of diverse cultural influences, travel becomes a tangible expression of commitment and shared dreams.

How do individuals in globalized relationships navigate the decision-making process of building a global home together? What role does travel play in shaping the vision of a shared future, and how does it contribute to the creation of a home that reflects the unique identity of the couple? The examination of building a global home together unveils the ways in which travel becomes an active and intentional part of the journey towards a shared life.

Coping with the Challenges of Travel:

While travel brings numerous joys, it also presents challenges that couples in globalized relationships must navigate. From logistical hurdles to the occasional travel-related stress, the exploration of coping with the challenges of travel delves into how couples overcome obstacles and use these experiences as opportunities for growth.

How do individuals in globalized relationships cope with the practical challenges of travel, such as jet lag, travel fatigue, or navigating unfamiliar environments? What role does effective communication and mutual support play in addressing the occasional stressors associated with travel? The examination of coping with the challenges of travel unveils the ways in which couples build resilience and strengthen their connection amidst the complexities of a globalized lifestyle.

Technological Facilitation of Distant Connections:

In the age of technology, travel is facilitated and complemented by virtual connections. The exploration of the technological facilitation of distant connections delves into how couples use digital platforms, video calls, and social media to stay connected when physical travel is not feasible. These virtual connections become a vital lifeline, allowing couples to maintain a sense of closeness despite geographical distances.

How do individuals in globalized relationships leverage technology to bridge the gap when physical travel is not possible? What role do virtual connections play in sustaining emotional intimacy and communication across borders? The examination of technological facilitation of distant connections unveils the ways in which digital tools become integral to the fabric of modern love stories.

Travel as a Catalyst for Personal Growth:

Beyond its impact on the relationship, travel becomes a catalyst for personal growth for individuals in globalized relationships. The exploration of travel as a catalyst for personal growth delves into how exposure to new cultures, perspectives, and environments contributes to the development of resilience, adaptability, and a broader worldview.

How does travel shape the personal growth of individuals in globalized relationships, and what lessons do they carry from each journey? What role does the continuous exploration of new landscapes play in fostering a sense of curiosity, open-mindedness, and self-discovery? The examination of travel as a catalyst for personal growth unveils the ways in which individuals in globalized relationships embark on a transformative journey not only as a couple but also as individuals with unique narratives and aspirations.

Conclusion: The Ever-Expanding Horizons of Love Through Travel:

As we conclude our exploration of the role of travel in modern love stories, we invite you to reflect on the stories, challenges, and enriching experiences presented in this chapter. From shared adventures to the intentional building of a global home, travel emerges as a dynamic and integral part of the narrative of globalized relationships.

Join us in the next chapter as we delve into the future trends of love and relationships, anticipating the ways in which technology, societal norms, and individual aspirations may continue to shape the evolving landscape of modern love stories.

Chapter 7: Future Trends in Love and Relationships
Emerging Trends in Love and Partnership

As we stand on the cusp of a new era, the landscape of love and partnerships is poised for transformation. Emerging trends in love and partnership reflect the evolving dynamics of our interconnected world, influenced by technological advancements, shifting societal norms, and the continuous quest for meaningful connections. This section explores the forefront of change, examining the emerging trends that are shaping the future of love in the 21st century.

Digital Dating and AI Matchmaking:

The digital age has revolutionized the way individuals connect romantically. Emerging trends indicate a continued reliance on digital dating platforms and the integration of artificial intelligence (AI) in matchmaking algorithms. How are AI technologies reshaping the landscape of dating, and what role do they play in enhancing compatibility assessments and predicting relationship success? The exploration of digital dating and AI matchmaking unveils the ways in which technology is becoming an increasingly sophisticated matchmaker in the quest for love.

Virtual Reality and Augmented Reality Experiences:

The immersive experiences offered by virtual reality (VR) and augmented reality (AR) are extending into the realm of romantic connections. Emerging trends suggest that couples may soon engage in virtual dates, exploring simulated environments together or creating shared augmented reality spaces. How are VR and AR technologies reshaping the way couples interact and create shared experiences, even when physically apart? The examination of virtual reality and augmented reality experiences delves into the ways in which technology is pushing the boundaries of virtual connections in the pursuit of love.

Sustainable and Conscious Relationships:

A growing awareness of environmental and social issues is influencing emerging trends in relationships. Sustainable and conscious partnerships are gaining prominence, with individuals seeking connections that align with their values and contribute to a positive impact on the world. How are sustainability and consciousness becoming integral aspects of relationship dynamics, influencing everything from lifestyle choices to shared goals? The exploration of sustainable and conscious relationships unveils the ways in which individuals are redefining what it means to build a meaningful connection in an era of heightened global awareness.

Polyamory and Non-Traditional Relationship Structures:

As societal norms continue to evolve, non-traditional relationship structures, including polyamory, are gaining acceptance. Emerging trends suggest that individuals are exploring diverse ways of forming connections, challenging traditional notions of monogamy. How are polyamorous and non-traditional relationship structures reshaping the landscape of love, and what role do communication and consent play in navigating these complex dynamics? The examination of polyamory and non-traditional relationship structures delves into the ways in which individuals are embracing a spectrum of relationship possibilities in the pursuit of authentic connections.

Integration of Biotechnology in Partner Selection:

Advancements in biotechnology, including genetic testing and analysis, are influencing emerging trends in partner selection. Individuals are exploring the integration of genetic compatibility assessments in the quest for long-lasting relationships. How are biotechnological advancements shaping the criteria for partner selection, and what ethical considerations arise in this era of genetic exploration? The exploration of the integration of biotechnology in partner selection unveils the ways in which science is becoming a factor in the pursuit of compatible and genetically aligned connections.

Long-Distance Relationships with Enhanced Connectivity:

The globalization of relationships is being further enhanced by emerging trends in long-distance connections. Technology is playing a pivotal role in fostering enhanced connectivity for couples separated by geographical distances. How are emerging technologies, such as high-quality video communication and virtual reality, redefining the dynamics of long-distance relationships? The examination of long-distance relationships with enhanced connectivity delves into the ways in which individuals are navigating the challenges of physical separation while fostering meaningful connections in the digital age.

AI Companions and Emotional Support Systems:

The integration of artificial intelligence is extending beyond matchmaking algorithms to include AI companions and emotional support systems. Emerging trends suggest that individuals may turn to AI for companionship and emotional support, blurring the lines between human and artificial connections. How are AI companions shaping the landscape of emotional support, and what implications do these developments have for the future of human relationships? The exploration of AI companions and emotional support systems unveils the ways in which technology is becoming a source of comfort and connection in the pursuit of emotional well-being.

Shift in Attitudes Toward Marriage and Commitment:

Attitudes toward marriage and commitment are undergoing a shift, with emerging trends indicating a reevaluation of traditional expectations. Individuals are exploring diverse paths, including delayed marriage, cohabitation without marriage, or even choosing to remain single. How are changing societal norms influencing attitudes toward marriage and long-term commitment, and what role does individual agency play in shaping these choices? The examination of the shift in attitudes toward marriage and commitment delves into the ways in which individuals are navigating the evolving landscape of partnership in the 21st century.

Exploration of Relationship Contracts and Agreements:

In the quest for transparency and mutual understanding, emerging trends include the exploration of relationship contracts and agreements. Couples are increasingly considering formalized agreements that outline expectations, boundaries, and responsibilities within the partnership. How are relationship contracts reshaping the way individuals approach commitment, and what role does clear communication play in establishing these agreements? The exploration of relationship contracts and agreements unveils the ways in which individuals are proactively shaping the terms of their connections in a quest for clarity and mutual respect.

Increased Focus on Mental Health and Relationship Wellness:

A growing emphasis on mental health and overall relationship wellness is influencing emerging trends in love and partnerships. Individuals are recognizing the importance of prioritizing emotional well-being and seeking connections that contribute positively to mental health. How are conversations around mental health becoming integral to relationship dynamics, and what role do open communication and support systems play in fostering relationship wellness? The examination of increased focus on mental health and relationship wellness delves into the ways in which individuals are redefining success in love beyond traditional benchmarks.

Embracing Fluidity in Gender and Sexual Identity:

As societal norms evolve, emerging trends indicate an increasing embrace of fluidity in gender and sexual identity within relationships. Individuals are challenging traditional labels and exploring a spectrum of identities and expressions. How are changing perceptions of gender and sexual identity influencing the dynamics of love, and what role does acceptance and inclusivity play in fostering authentic connections? The exploration of embracing fluidity in gender and sexual identity unveils the ways in which individuals are celebrating the diversity of human expression in the realm of love.

Conclusion: Navigating the Uncharted Waters of Future Love:

As we conclude our exploration of emerging trends in love and partnership, we invite you to reflect on the dynamic shifts, challenges, and possibilities presented in this chapter. The future of love is a canvas awaiting new strokes, shaped by the interplay of technology, societal values, and individual choices.

Join us in the final chapter as we reflect on the contemporary expressions of love, navigating the complexities of modern relationships, and embracing the fluidity and diversity that characterize love in the 21st century.

Technology's Future Impact on Love

As we peer into the horizon of the future, the role of technology in shaping the landscape of love becomes increasingly profound. Technological advancements continue to redefine how individuals connect, form relationships, and navigate the intricacies of modern love. This section explores the anticipated future impact of technology on love, examining the potential trends and transformations that await us in the evolving tapestry of human connections.

AI and Advanced Matchmaking Algorithms:

The future of love is intricately intertwined with artificial intelligence (AI), promising a new era of sophisticated matchmaking. Anticipated advancements include AI algorithms that go beyond mere compatibility assessments, delving into nuanced understanding of individual preferences, communication styles, and emotional needs. How might AI-driven matchmaking redefine the way individuals find compatible partners, and what ethical considerations arise in the era of AI-assisted love? The exploration of AI and advanced matchmaking algorithms unveils the potential for technology to become an even more intuitive and insightful matchmaker in the quest for love.

Virtual Reality (VR) and Augmented Reality (AR) in Romantic Experiences:

As the line between physical and virtual realities continues to blur, the future of love is likely to embrace immersive experiences facilitated by virtual reality (VR) and augmented reality (AR). Envision a world where couples can share virtual spaces, attend simulated events together, or even embark on virtual vacations. How might VR and AR redefine romantic experiences and deepen emotional connections, especially for couples separated by geographical distances? The examination of VR and AR in romantic experiences delves into the potential for technology to create a new dimension of shared moments and adventures in the pursuit of love.

Biometric Data and Personalized Relationship Insights:

The future holds the promise of leveraging biometric data and wearable technology to gain personalized insights into relationships. Imagine a scenario where devices can track physiological responses, such as heart rate and skin conductivity, providing individuals with real-time feedback on their emotional states. How might the integration of biometric data enhance self-awareness and communication within relationships, offering a deeper understanding of emotional dynamics? The exploration of biometric data and personalized relationship insights unveils the potential for technology to contribute to emotional intelligence and relational self-discovery.

Blockchain Technology for Trust and Transparency:

In an era where trust and transparency are paramount, blockchain technology emerges as a potential game-changer in the future of love. Anticipated trends include the use of blockchain for secure and transparent record-keeping in relationships, from dating histories to shared commitments. How might blockchain foster trust in online interactions and redefine the way individuals approach transparency in matters of the heart? The examination of blockchain technology for trust and transparency explores the potential for technology to be a catalyst for building more secure and accountable connections.

Emotional AI Companions and Support Systems:

As AI becomes increasingly sophisticated, the future envisions emotional AI companions and support systems playing a more integral role in individuals' lives. These AI entities could provide companionship, emotional support, and even assist in relationship counseling. How might emotional AI companions contribute to individuals' well-being and offer a new avenue for emotional connection in the absence of traditional relationships? The exploration of emotional AI companions and support systems unveils the potential for technology to become a source of comfort and understanding in the complex landscape of modern love.

Quantum Computing and Relationship Predictions:

The advent of quantum computing holds the potential to revolutionize relationship predictions by processing vast amounts of data at unprecedented speeds. Anticipated trends include the use of quantum algorithms to analyze complex relationship dynamics, offering insights into long-term compatibility and potential challenges. How might quantum computing enhance our understanding of the intricacies of human connections, and what ethical considerations arise in predicting the future of relationships? The examination of quantum computing and relationship predictions delves into the potential for technology to provide more nuanced and accurate insights into the trajectories of love.

Biotechnological Enhancements for Genetic Compatibility:

The future of love may witness the integration of biotechnological enhancements in the quest for genetic compatibility. From advanced genetic testing to potential interventions, individuals may explore ways to optimize biological compatibility in their relationships. How might biotechnological advancements influence partner selection and redefine the criteria for genetic compatibility in the pursuit of lasting connections? The exploration of biotechnological enhancements for genetic compatibility unveils the potential for technology to become a factor in shaping the biological dimensions of love.

Social Media Evolution and Influences on Relationship Dynamics:

As social media continues to evolve, its impact on relationship dynamics is expected to undergo further transformations. Anticipated trends include new forms of digital expression of love, virtual reality social platforms, and heightened awareness of the effects of online presence on relationships. How might social media shape the narrative of modern love in the future, and what considerations should individuals keep in mind as they navigate the digital realm of relationships? The examination of social media evolution and influences on relationship dynamics delves into the potential for technology to redefine the way individuals express, perceive, and maintain their connections in the digital age.

Robotics and Humanoid Companionship:

The integration of robotics into the realm of love suggests the potential for humanoid companionship in the future. From robotic partners designed for emotional connection to AI-driven humanoid assistants, individuals may explore new dimensions of companionship beyond traditional human relationships. How might robotics redefine the concept of companionship, and what ethical considerations arise in the development of AI-driven humanoid partners? The exploration of robotics and humanoid companionship unveils the potential for technology to offer alternative forms of connection and support in the pursuit of love.

Privacy and Security Measures in Online Relationships:

With the increasing prevalence of online relationships, the future is likely to witness a heightened focus on privacy and security measures. Anticipated trends include advanced encryption, secure authentication processes, and enhanced protection against cyber threats in the realm of online dating and digital connections. How might the emphasis on privacy and security measures contribute to a safer and more trustworthy online environment for individuals seeking love? The examination of privacy and security measures in online relationships delves into the potential for technology to address concerns and build confidence in the digital landscape of love.

Integration of Virtual and Physical Realities:

The future of love holds the promise of a more seamless integration between virtual and physical realities. Anticipated trends include technologies that allow individuals to transition effortlessly between digital and physical spaces, blurring the lines between online and offline interactions. How might the integration of virtual and physical realities redefine the way individuals experience and navigate love, especially in a world where digital connections play an increasingly significant role? The exploration of the integration of virtual and physical realities unveils the potential for technology to create a more fluid and interconnected experience of modern love.

Conclusion: Navigating the Technological Frontier of Love:

As we conclude our exploration of the future impact of technology on love, we invite you to reflect on the exciting possibilities, challenges, and ethical considerations presented in this chapter. The intersection of technology and love is a frontier awaiting exploration, where innovation has the potential to reshape the very fabric of human connections.

Join us in the final chapter as we reflect on the overarching themes of love in the 21st century, embracing the complexities, diversities, and evolving narratives that define the landscape of modern relationships.

Changing Views on Marriage and Commitment

The institution of marriage, once a societal cornerstone, is undergoing a profound transformation in the evolving landscape of love and relationships. As we navigate the future, changing views on marriage and commitment signal a shift in societal norms and individual aspirations. This section delves into the emerging trends and perspectives that are redefining the very essence of marriage and commitment in the 21st century.

The Evolution of Marriage:

The concept of marriage has evolved throughout history, shaped by cultural, religious, and societal influences. In the future, we anticipate a continuation of this evolution, with individuals challenging traditional notions and exploring new paradigms of marital relationships. How might the institution of marriage adapt to reflect the changing values, expectations, and aspirations of individuals in the coming years? The exploration of the evolution of marriage unveils the ways in which this timeless institution is reshaping itself to align with contemporary ideals.

Delaying Marriage and Prioritizing Individual Growth:

One noticeable trend in changing views on marriage is the inclination to delay this commitment in favor of individual growth and self-discovery. As individuals focus on personal development, career pursuits, and the exploration of diverse life experiences, the traditional timeline for marriage is being reconsidered. How might the emphasis on individual growth impact the timing and dynamics of marriage, and what role does personal fulfillment play in shaping future commitments? The examination of delaying marriage and prioritizing individual growth delves into the ways in which evolving perspectives on personal development influence the journey towards matrimony.

The Rise of Non-Traditional Commitment Models:

In the future, non-traditional commitment models are gaining acceptance, challenging the conventional understanding of marriage. From cohabitation without marriage to explorations of polyamory and open relationships, individuals are seeking relationship structures that align with their values and desires. How might the rise of non-traditional commitment models redefine the parameters of love and commitment, and what considerations come into play in navigating these alternative paths? The exploration of non-traditional commitment models unveils the ways in which individuals are shaping new narratives for committed partnerships.

Fluidity in Relationship Definitions:

The future of love envisions a greater fluidity in how individuals define their relationships. Terms such as "partnership," "companionship," and "life commitment" are gaining prominence, offering individuals the flexibility to express their connection in ways that resonate with their unique circumstances. How might the shift towards fluidity in relationship definitions impact societal perceptions, and what role does language play in shaping the understanding of committed partnerships? The examination of fluidity in relationship definitions delves into the ways in which individuals are embracing diverse expressions of love and commitment.

Reimagining Marital Roles and Responsibilities:

Changing views on marriage include a reimagining of traditional roles and responsibilities within marital partnerships. As gender norms evolve and expectations around equality gain traction, couples are exploring ways to co-create their lives without being bound by traditional gendered roles. How might the reimagining of marital roles contribute to more equitable and fulfilling partnerships, and what challenges and opportunities arise in this transformative process? The exploration of reimagining marital roles and responsibilities unveils the ways in which individuals are reshaping the dynamics of shared life within the institution of marriage.

Focus on Emotional Connection and Intimacy:

The future of marriage is characterized by a heightened emphasis on emotional connection and intimacy. Couples are prioritizing the quality of their emotional bond, valuing open communication, vulnerability, and mutual understanding. How might the focus on emotional connection redefine the benchmarks of a successful marriage, and what role does intimacy play in sustaining long-term commitment? The examination of the focus on emotional connection and intimacy delves into the ways in which individuals are elevating the emotional dimensions of their marital relationships.

Individual Agency in Choosing Commitment:

As societal expectations evolve, the future sees a greater emphasis on individual agency in choosing commitment. The decision to marry or commit is becoming a more personal and intentional choice, driven by individual values, aspirations, and desires. How might individual agency reshape the landscape of commitment, and what considerations do individuals weigh when navigating the decision to commit to a lifelong partnership? The exploration of individual agency in choosing commitment unveils the ways in which individuals are taking an active role in defining the trajectory of their relationships.

Legal and Social Recognition of Diverse Unions:

Changing views on marriage extend to the legal and social recognition of diverse unions. The future envisions a more inclusive approach, where various forms of committed partnerships, including same-sex marriages and non-traditional unions, are acknowledged and celebrated. How might the broader recognition of diverse unions contribute to a more inclusive and accepting society, and what role do legal frameworks play in shaping the narrative of marriage in the years to come? The examination of legal and social recognition of diverse unions delves into the ways in which evolving perspectives on love extend to the broader societal landscape.

The Role of Technology in Shaping Commitment:

In the digital age, technology is playing an increasingly significant role in shaping views on commitment. From online dating platforms facilitating connections to virtual ceremonies celebrating unions, technology is influencing how individuals approach commitment. How might technology continue to redefine the process of finding and sustaining committed partnerships, and what challenges and opportunities arise in this technologically mediated landscape of love? The exploration of the role of technology in shaping commitment unveils the ways in which digital innovations impact the dynamics of modern relationships.

Evolving Attitudes Toward Monogamy:

Attitudes toward monogamy are evolving, with individuals challenging the traditional assumption that monogamous relationships are the only valid form of commitment. The future sees a more nuanced understanding of monogamy, where individuals may explore consensual non-monogamy or consensual monogamy based on personal preferences. How might evolving attitudes toward monogamy reshape the expectations and negotiations within committed partnerships, and what considerations arise in navigating diverse approaches to fidelity? The examination of evolving attitudes toward monogamy delves into the ways in which individuals are redefining the boundaries of commitment.

Balancing Autonomy and Togetherness:

A key theme in changing views on marriage is the delicate balance between autonomy and togetherness. Couples are seeking a middle ground that allows each partner to maintain a sense of individuality while fostering a strong sense of partnership. How might the pursuit of this balance impact relationship satisfaction and the longevity of commitments, and what strategies do couples employ to navigate the complexities of autonomy and togetherness? The exploration of balancing autonomy and togetherness unveils the ways in which individuals are redefining the dynamics of interdependence within committed partnerships.

The Impact of External Pressures on Commitment:

External pressures, including societal expectations, familial influences, and economic considerations, have historically played a role in shaping views on marriage. In the future, individuals may navigate these external pressures with greater discernment, prioritizing authentic connection over societal norms. How might changing attitudes toward external pressures impact the decision to commit, and what role does resilience play in facing societal expectations? The examination of the impact of external pressures on commitment delves into the ways in which individuals are asserting their autonomy in the face of external influences.

Conclusion: Embracing the Evolution of Commitment:

As we conclude our exploration of changing views on marriage and commitment, we invite you to reflect on the dynamic shifts, challenges, and possibilities presented in this chapter. The future of commitment is an evolving narrative, shaped by the interplay of individual choices, societal values, and the ever-changing landscape of love.

Join us in the final chapter as we reflect on contemporary expressions of love, navigating the complexities of modern relationships, and embracing the fluidity and diversity that characterize love in the 21st century.

Anticipating the Evolution of Modern Love

In the unfolding tapestry of human connections, the anticipation of the evolution of modern love is a journey into uncharted territory. As we look ahead, the dynamics of love and relationships are poised for transformation, shaped by societal shifts, technological innovations, and the continuous reevaluation of individual desires. This section explores the multifaceted dimensions of anticipating the evolution of modern love, examining the emerging trends and potential trajectories that may redefine the very essence of how we love and connect in the future.

The Intersection of Technology and Intimacy:

At the heart of anticipating the evolution of modern love lies the intricate dance between technology and intimacy. The future envisions a seamless integration where technology enhances rather than hinders the depth of human connection. From virtual reality experiences that simulate physical presence to advanced communication tools fostering emotional intimacy, how might technology become a catalyst for deeper and more meaningful connections? The exploration of the intersection of technology and intimacy unveils the potential for a harmonious coexistence, where digital innovations enrich the fabric of modern love.

Inclusive Narratives of Love:

Anticipating the evolution of modern love involves embracing more inclusive narratives that reflect the diverse spectrum of human connections. As societal norms continue to shift, the future sees a celebration of love in all its forms— regardless of gender, sexual orientation, or relationship structure. How might inclusive narratives of love contribute to a more accepting and understanding society, and what role do individuals play in shaping these evolving narratives? The examination of inclusive narratives of love delves into the ways in which the future envisions a more expansive and encompassing understanding of human connection.

Sustainable and Mindful Relationships:

The evolution of modern love is intertwined with a growing awareness of sustainability, not just for the planet but also for the well-being of individuals within relationships. Future trends suggest a focus on mindful connections, where individuals prioritize the health of the relationship and the mutual growth of partners. How might the emphasis on sustainable and mindful relationships shape the choices individuals make in the pursuit of lasting love, and what considerations come into play in nurturing a relationship with intentionality? The exploration of sustainable and mindful relationships unveils the ways in which the future envisions a more conscious and deliberate approach to love.

Shifts in Relationship Definitions:

As we anticipate the evolution of modern love, we foresee a departure from rigid relationship definitions towards a more fluid and customizable landscape. Individuals are increasingly empowered to define the parameters of their connections, using language that resonates with their unique experiences. How might shifts in relationship definitions reflect the changing dynamics of love, and what implications do these evolving definitions have for societal perceptions? The examination of shifts in relationship definitions delves into the ways in which individuals are reclaiming agency in shaping the narratives of their love stories.

Augmented Emotional Intelligence:

The future of love involves an augmentation of emotional intelligence through the integration of technology and psychological insights. Anticipated trends include the development of tools that enhance individuals' understanding of their own emotions and the emotions of their partners. How might augmented emotional intelligence contribute to more empathetic and resilient relationships, and what ethical considerations arise in the pursuit of emotional enhancement? The exploration of augmented emotional intelligence unveils the potential for technology to play a role in fostering deeper emotional connections in the evolving landscape of modern love.

Navigating Virtual and Physical Realities:

Anticipating the evolution of modern love requires navigating the seamless integration of virtual and physical realities. As individuals continue to forge connections in digital spaces, the future sees an increasing fluidity in transitioning between online and offline interactions. How might the ability to navigate virtual and physical realities redefine the nature of relationships, and what challenges and opportunities arise in this interconnected landscape? The examination of navigating virtual and physical realities delves into the ways in which individuals are mastering the art of balancing digital connections with tangible, real-world experiences.

Customized Relationship Agreements:

The future envisions a departure from one-size-fits-all relationship structures towards customized agreements that reflect the unique needs and desires of individuals. Anticipated trends include the exploration of relationship contracts and agreements that explicitly outline expectations, boundaries, and shared goals. How might the shift towards customized relationship agreements empower individuals to create partnerships that align with their values, and what role does clear communication play in establishing these personalized contracts? The exploration of customized relationship agreements unveils the ways in which the future embraces a more tailored and intentional approach to commitment.

Conscious Integration of Technology:

As we look ahead, the conscious integration of technology into the fabric of modern love becomes a pivotal theme. Rather than being passive consumers of technological advancements, individuals are anticipated to adopt a more intentional and mindful approach to their digital interactions. How might the conscious integration of technology enhance the quality of relationships, and what considerations come into play as individuals navigate the digital landscape of love? The examination of the conscious integration of technology delves into the ways in which the future envisions a harmonious relationship between humanity and digital innovation.

The Role of Education in Relationship Skills:

Anticipating the evolution of modern love involves recognizing the role of education in nurturing relationship skills. Future trends suggest a greater emphasis on educational programs that equip individuals with the tools to navigate the complexities of modern relationships. How might educational initiatives contribute to the development of healthier and more resilient partnerships, and what subjects should be included in relationship education curricula? The exploration of the role of education in relationship skills unveils the potential for a more informed and prepared generation in matters of the heart.

Ethical Considerations in Love Technology:

As technology becomes an integral part of modern love, ethical considerations take center stage. Anticipated trends include a heightened awareness of the ethical implications of using technology in the realm of relationships. How might individuals and society at large navigate the ethical considerations surrounding love technology, and what safeguards should be put in place to ensure responsible innovation? The examination of ethical considerations in love technology delves into the ways in which the future envisions a balance between technological progress and ethical responsibility.

Cross-Cultural Influences on Love:

The evolution of modern love is enriched by cross-cultural influences, fostering a global tapestry of diverse expressions and practices. As individuals connect across borders and cultures, the future sees a blending of traditions, values, and perspectives on love. How might cross-cultural influences contribute to a more interconnected and enriched landscape of modern love, and what challenges and rewards arise in navigating relationships that span diverse cultural backgrounds? The exploration of cross-cultural influences on love unveils the ways in which the future embraces a more expansive and globally interconnected understanding of human connections.

Conclusion: Embracing the Uncharted Future of Love:

As we conclude our exploration of anticipating the evolution of modern love, we invite you to reflect on the myriad possibilities, challenges, and exciting trajectories that lie ahead. The future of love is a canvas waiting for the brushstrokes of human experience, where innovation, intentionality, and a profound understanding of human nature converge to shape the narratives of our shared journey.

Join us in the final chapter as we reflect on the overarching themes of love in the 21st century, navigating the complexities of modern relationships, and embracing the fluidity and diversity that characterize love today.

Conclusion: Love in the 21st Century
Reflecting on Contemporary Expressions of Love

As we stand at the crossroads of the 21st century, the landscape of love unfolds before us in ways unprecedented and multifaceted. This concluding chapter invites us to take a reflective journey through the diverse expressions, evolving dynamics, and transformative forces that shape love in the contemporary era. From the impact of technology to the redefinition of traditional norms, we delve into the intricacies of modern relationships, acknowledging the beauty and complexity that define love in the 21st century.

The Technological Tapestry of Love:

Contemporary expressions of love are intricately woven into the technological tapestry that envelops our daily lives. The advent of digital platforms, dating apps, and virtual communication tools has fundamentally altered how we initiate, sustain, and even end romantic relationships. Reflecting on the technological influences on modern expressions of love requires an exploration of the nuances and challenges that accompany these innovations.

Technology has not only expanded the avenues through which we connect with potential partners but has also introduced novel ways to express affection and maintain intimacy. The immediacy of communication, the visual richness of video calls, and the shared experiences facilitated by virtual spaces have all contributed to a reimagining of love in the digital age.

However, this technological revolution in love is not without its pitfalls. The ubiquity of dating apps has raised questions about the commodification of relationships, as individuals navigate a sea of profiles in search of their ideal match. The paradox of choice, coupled with the illusion of endless possibilities, poses challenges in cultivating meaningful connections. As we reflect on contemporary expressions of love, we must confront the dichotomy of technology as both an enabler and a disruptor of modern romance.

The Shifting Sands of Relationship Dynamics:

Navigating the complexities of modern relationships requires an acknowledgment of the shifting sands upon which they are built. Evolving notions of love and commitment have given rise to a more fluid and personalized approach to partnerships. Reflecting on the changing dynamics of romantic relationships involves an exploration of the diverse structures and arrangements that define love in the 21st century.

Traditional paradigms of monogamy and marriage are being reexamined, with individuals seeking relationship models that align with their values and aspirations. The evolving landscape of gender roles has further contributed to the transformation of relationship dynamics, fostering partnerships based on equality and mutual understanding.

Yet, with this evolution comes a reevaluation of individualism's impact on partnership. The emphasis on personal fulfillment and autonomy, while empowering, can also introduce challenges in balancing the needs of the self with the demands of a shared life. As we reflect on contemporary expressions of love, we must navigate the delicate equilibrium between individual growth and the cultivation of a strong, interconnected bond.

The Influence of External Forces on Love:

Contemporary expressions of love are not formed in isolation but are subject to the influence of external forces. From the celebrity-driven trends that shape romantic ideals to the impact of social media on public perceptions of love, external factors play a significant role in shaping our understanding of romantic relationships. Reflecting on the influence of external forces on love involves an examination of the subtle ways in which societal expectations and pop culture shape our desires and aspirations.

Celebrity relationships, amplified by the pervasive reach of social media, create aspirational narratives that influence our perceptions of love and romance. The commodification of love through celebrity-endorsed brands further intertwines the realms of fame and romantic ideals. As we reflect on contemporary expressions of love, we must critically engage with the narratives presented by external influences, recognizing their power to shape our desires and expectations.

Love Across Boundaries:

Contemporary expressions of love transcend geographical constraints, ushering in an era where relationships unfold across time zones and cultural divides. The advent of virtual celebrations and the joys and challenges of long-distance relationships highlight the globalized nature of modern love. Reflecting on love in the age of globalization necessitates an exploration of the ways in which individuals navigate the complexities of love that transcends borders.

Cross-cultural relationships and international love stories enrich the narrative of contemporary expressions of love, introducing a tapestry of diverse experiences and perspectives. However, the challenges inherent in globalized love, including the impact of distance on intimacy and the need for effective communication across cultural nuances, require careful consideration. As we reflect on love in the age of globalization, we recognize the potential for both enriching connections and the complexities that arise when love knows no geographical boundaries.

The Psychosocial Landscape of Love:

Contemporary expressions of love are intricately intertwined with the psychosocial landscape of the 21st century. The advent of online dating and the influence of social media have redefined how individuals perceive themselves in the context of romantic relationships. Reflecting on the psychology of love today involves an exploration of the ways in which digital communication shapes self-perception and emotional intimacy.

The impact of social media on self-perception in relationships introduces a nuanced layer to the psychological dynamics of modern love. From curated online personas to the implications of constant connectivity, individuals grapple with the intersections of technology and psychology. As we reflect on the psychosocial landscape of love, we must confront the implications of digital communication on emotional intimacy, acknowledging both its potential benefits and pitfalls.

Love's Evolution in a Globalized World:

Contemporary expressions of love are deeply entwined with the evolution of relationships in a globalized world. The changing views on marriage and commitment reflect a broader shift in societal norms and individual aspirations. Reflecting on love's evolution in a globalized world involves an exploration of the emerging trends that anticipate the future of love and partnerships.

The rise of non-traditional commitment models, the focus on emotional connection and intimacy, and the reimagining of marital roles contribute to a narrative of love that transcends traditional boundaries. As we reflect on love's evolution in a globalized world, we must anticipate the continued impact of technology, changing views on monogamy, and the conscious integration of cultural influences on the future of love.

Embracing the Future Trends of Love:

Contemporary expressions of love set the stage for embracing the future trends that will shape the landscape of relationships. Anticipating the evolution of modern love involves navigating the intersections of technology, inclusivity, and mindful connections. Reflecting on the potential trajectories of love invites us to explore the ways in which technology can enhance emotional intelligence, the role of education in nurturing relationship skills, and the ethical considerations that accompany love technology.

As we embrace the future trends of love, we recognize the importance of customization in relationship agreements, the navigation of virtual and physical realities, and the conscious integration of technology into the fabric of modern relationships. Reflecting on contemporary expressions of love requires an active engagement with the possibilities and challenges that the future holds, recognizing that the narrative of love is an ever-evolving story written by the collective experiences of individuals navigating the complexities of the 21st century.

Conclusion: Navigating the Complexities of Modern Love:

In concluding our exploration of contemporary expressions of love, we find ourselves at the intersection of tradition and innovation, individuality and interconnectedness, and the timeless quest for meaningful connections. Navigating the complexities of modern love involves a continuous process of self-discovery, adaptation, and an openness to the diverse expressions that love can take.

As we reflect on the technological influences, changing dynamics, external influences, globalized nature, psychosocial landscape, and evolving views on love, we acknowledge the beauty of diversity in how individuals experience and express love. Love in the 21st century is a mosaic of experiences, a tapestry woven with threads of tradition and threads of innovation.

Embracing the Fluidity and Diversity of Love Today:

In the final analysis, contemporary expressions of love call us to embrace the fluidity and diversity that characterize love in the 21st century. Each love story is unique, shaped by personal histories, cultural contexts, and the ever-changing landscape of human connection. Reflecting on love today encourages us to celebrate the myriad ways in which individuals navigate relationships, express affection, and find meaning in the tapestry of love that binds us all.

As we conclude this exploration of love in the 21st century, we extend an invitation to continue the journey, to explore new chapters, and to contribute to the ongoing narrative of love in our ever-evolving world. Love, in all its forms, remains a profound and enduring aspect of the human experience—a journey that unfolds with each heartbeat, creating a symphony of emotions, connections, and shared moments that transcend the boundaries of time and technology.

May the exploration of contemporary expressions of love inspire conversations, foster understanding, and illuminate the path forward as we navigate the complex, beautiful, and ever-changing landscape of modern relationships.

Navigating the Complexities of Modern Relationships

In the tapestry of human connection, the concluding chapter of our exploration beckons us to confront the intricacies and nuances that define the landscape of modern relationships. As we navigate the complexities of love in the 21st century, we find ourselves in a dynamic interplay of tradition and innovation, individuality and interconnectedness, and the timeless quest for meaningful connections. This section delves into the multifaceted challenges and triumphs that mark the journey of navigating the complexities of modern relationships.

The Dance of Tradition and Innovation:

At the heart of navigating the complexities of modern relationships is the delicate dance between tradition and innovation. The 21st century presents a paradoxical landscape where age-old notions of love and commitment coexist with the relentless march of technological progress. How do individuals reconcile traditional values with the ever-evolving dynamics of modern romance, and what tensions arise in the interplay between the old and the new?

The integration of technology into the fabric of relationships introduces both conveniences and complexities. Dating apps offer unprecedented access to potential partners, yet they also pose challenges in discerning genuine connections amid the digital noise. Virtual communication tools bridge geographical gaps but may test the depth of emotional intimacy. Navigating this intricate dance requires a conscious awareness of how tradition and innovation intersect in shaping the contours of modern love.

Individuality and Interconnectedness:

Navigating the complexities of modern relationships entails striking a delicate balance between individuality and interconnectedness. The emphasis on personal growth, autonomy, and self-discovery is a hallmark of contemporary romance. Yet, this pursuit of individual fulfillment coexists with the profound yearning for shared experiences, emotional intimacy, and mutual understanding.

Individuality in modern relationships is not a challenge to be overcome but a dynamic force to be embraced. How do partners honor each other's individual journeys while fostering a sense of togetherness? What negotiation is required to ensure that personal aspirations harmonize with shared goals? As we navigate the delicate interplay of individuality and interconnectedness, we uncover the richness that arises when two unique souls intertwine their paths in the journey of love.

The Influence of External Factors:

External factors cast a considerable shadow on the path of modern relationships, influencing the choices individuals make and shaping societal expectations. The constant gaze of social media, the allure of celebrity-driven romantic ideals, and the pervasive impact of pop culture all contribute to the external narrative of love. Navigating the complexities of modern relationships involves a critical examination of how external influences shape perceptions and impact the dynamics of intimate connections.

The curated images presented on social media platforms create a narrative that often diverges from the complexities of real-life relationships. Celebrity relationships, adorned with glamour and public scrutiny, cast long shadows on public perceptions of what constitutes an ideal partnership. How do individuals navigate the external pressures exerted by these influences, and what strategies are employed to maintain authenticity amid the curated images of love presented in the public domain?

Globalization and Its Impact:

The interconnected world of the 21st century, fueled by globalization, significantly influences the landscape of modern relationships. The opportunities and challenges posed by a globalized society require individuals to navigate love across borders, cultures, and time zones. How do couples navigate the complexities of globalized love, embracing the richness of cross-cultural connections while facing the practical challenges of distance and differing societal norms?

Globalization introduces a tapestry of diverse perspectives and experiences to the narrative of modern relationships. Cross-cultural relationships contribute to a broader understanding of love, challenging individuals to confront biases and preconceptions. As we navigate the impact of globalization on modern relationships, we uncover the potential for enriched connections that transcend geographical boundaries.

The Intricacies of the Psychosocial Landscape:

The psychosocial landscape of modern relationships is marked by the profound impact of technology on self-perception, emotional intimacy, and the very nature of human connection. The omnipresence of social media introduces complexities in how individuals perceive themselves within the context of romantic relationships. The immediacy of digital communication alters the dynamics of emotional intimacy, shaping the psychosocial landscape in ways both profound and subtle.

Navigating the intricacies of the psychosocial landscape involves a reflective journey into the effects of digital communication on self-esteem, jealousy, and trust within relationships. How do individuals balance the benefits of constant connectivity with the potential pitfalls of comparison and perceived inadequacy? As we navigate this complex terrain, we unravel the layers of the psychosocial landscape, understanding the nuances that shape the emotional dynamics of modern love.

The Changing Views on Love and Commitment:

The changing views on love and commitment in the 21st century reflect a broader shift in societal norms and individual aspirations. Evolving notions of monogamy, redefined gender roles, and the emphasis on personal fulfillment contribute to a reimagining of what constitutes a committed partnership. Navigating the changing landscape of love involves an exploration of the diverse relationship structures that individuals are increasingly embracing.

The journey of navigating changing views on love requires an open-minded approach to non-traditional commitment models. How do individuals negotiate evolving definitions of monogamy, and what role does open communication play in aligning expectations within partnerships? As we navigate the changing views on love and commitment, we uncover the potential for more inclusive and diverse expressions of romantic connections.

Conclusion: The Ongoing Journey of Love:

In concluding our exploration of navigating the complexities of modern relationships, we find ourselves at the crossroads of tradition and innovation, individuality and interconnectedness, and the constant negotiation between personal growth and shared experiences. The journey of love in the 21st century is not a linear path but a dynamic, ongoing process of adaptation, learning, and rediscovery.

As individuals navigate the complexities of modern relationships, they become architects of their own love stories, crafting narratives that reflect the unique contours of their journeys. The challenges posed by technology, external influences, globalization, the psychosocial landscape, and changing views on love are not obstacles to overcome but opportunities for growth, understanding, and resilience.

May the exploration of navigating the complexities of modern relationships inspire individuals to engage in meaningful conversations, foster deeper connections, and approach the ongoing journey of love with curiosity and compassion. In the ever-evolving landscape of human connection, the navigation of modern relationships remains an art—a dance that unfolds with each step, creating a mosaic of experiences, challenges, and moments of profound connection.

Embracing the Fluidity and Diversity of Love Today

In the closing chapter of our exploration into the intricacies of modern love, we turn our gaze toward a profound aspect that defines the essence of relationships in the 21st century—the fluidity and diversity that permeate the spectrum of love. As we delve into the nuances of embracing the myriad expressions and forms that love takes today, we uncover a rich tapestry woven with threads of individuality, inclusivity, and the evolving dynamics of human connection.

Individual Narratives, Collective Symphony:

The beauty of love in the 21st century lies in the kaleidoscope of individual narratives that collectively compose a symphony of experiences. Each person brings a unique story to the table, shaped by personal histories, cultural backgrounds, and the interplay of individual values. Embracing the fluidity and diversity of love begins with an acknowledgment that there is no singular, prescriptive formula for romantic connections.

In a world where individuality is celebrated, couples navigate the delicate balance of honoring personal narratives while co-creating a shared story. The fluidity of love allows for constant evolution, where relationships are not bound by rigid expectations but are dynamic, adaptive entities that grow in tandem with the individuals involved.

Challenges and Celebrations of Inclusivity:

Embracing the fluidity of love inherently involves recognizing and navigating the challenges and celebrations that come with inclusivity. The 21st century has seen a seismic shift in societal perspectives on love, challenging traditional norms and fostering a more inclusive understanding of relationships. How do individuals navigate the complexities of diverse expressions of love, and what strategies are employed to foster understanding and acceptance?

Inclusivity in modern love extends beyond the boundaries of gender, orientation, and relationship structures. It encompasses a broader recognition of diverse cultural influences, individual aspirations, and non-traditional commitment models. As we explore the challenges and celebrations of inclusivity, we unravel the potential for deeper connections that emerge when love transcends societal expectations and embraces the richness of diversity.

Intersectionality in Love:

The fluidity and diversity of love intersect with the multifaceted dimensions of identity, creating a tapestry where love is not confined to singular narratives. Intersectionality, the interconnected nature of social categorizations such as race, class, and gender, shapes the experiences of individuals within the landscape of love. How do factors such as race, ethnicity, and socioeconomic status influence the dynamics of romantic relationships, and how can couples navigate the intersections of identity within the context of love?

Acknowledging intersectionality in love involves an awareness of the unique challenges faced by individuals at the crossroads of different social categories. It requires an intentional effort to create spaces within relationships that foster open dialogue, empathy, and a shared commitment to dismantling systemic barriers. Embracing the fluidity of love in an intersectional context encourages couples to explore the richness that arises when diverse perspectives converge.

Technological Innovation and Relationship Customization:

The fluidity of love in the 21st century is intricately intertwined with technological innovation, offering unprecedented opportunities for relationship customization. Dating apps, virtual communication tools, and online platforms enable individuals to tailor their romantic experiences according to their preferences and values. How does technology contribute to the customization of modern relationships, and what considerations are vital in navigating the intersection of technology and intimacy?

Embracing the fluidity of love in the digital age involves a nuanced understanding of the role technology plays in shaping romantic connections. While technology provides avenues for customization, it also poses challenges such as the commodification of relationships and the impact of constant connectivity on intimacy. Navigating this intersection requires couples to engage in open communication, establish boundaries, and consciously integrate technology into the fabric of their relationships.

Fluidity in Relationship Structures:

The fluidity of love today is reflected in the evolving landscape of relationship structures. Non-traditional commitment models, open relationships, and polyamory challenge conventional notions of monogamy and redefine the parameters of romantic connections. How do individuals navigate the complexities of diverse relationship structures, and what role does open communication play in establishing mutual understanding and consent?

Embracing the fluidity of relationship structures involves transcending societal expectations and embracing models that align with the values and preferences of individuals involved. It requires a departure from rigid norms and an openness to exploring relationship structures that prioritize consent, communication, and mutual respect. The evolving dynamics of modern relationships invite individuals to actively participate in co-creating relationship models that honor the fluidity of love.

Embracing Change and Adaptation:

The fluidity of love necessitates an inherent capacity to embrace change and adapt to evolving circumstances. In a world where constant transformation is the norm, couples find resilience in their ability to navigate the ebb and flow of relationships. How do individuals cultivate adaptability within the context of love, and what practices contribute to the ongoing growth and development of relationships?

Embracing change in modern relationships involves an openness to learning, unlearning, and redefining expectations. It invites individuals to approach challenges as opportunities for growth and to view the evolution of love as a continuous journey. The capacity to adapt requires effective communication, emotional intelligence, and a shared commitment to navigating the complexities of love with curiosity and resilience.

Celebrating Love in All Its Forms:

At the heart of embracing the fluidity and diversity of love is a celebration of love in all its forms. Whether it manifests as a traditional partnership, an unconventional relationship structure, or a connection that defies categorization, love remains a powerful and transformative force. How can individuals actively contribute to the celebration of diverse expressions of love, fostering an environment where all forms of romantic connections are acknowledged and respected?

Celebrating love in all its forms involves dismantling stigmas, challenging biases, and actively advocating for inclusivity. It requires a commitment to creating spaces where individuals feel seen, heard, and valued in their unique expressions of love. The celebration of love as a diverse and fluid experience contributes to the creation of a more compassionate, understanding, and accepting society.

Conclusion: A Tapestry of Love Unfolding:

As we conclude our exploration of embracing the fluidity and diversity of love today, we find ourselves immersed in a tapestry of connections that transcend boundaries and defy rigid definitions. The journey of love in the 21st century is not a linear path but a dynamic, ever-unfolding narrative written by the collective experiences of individuals navigating the complexities of human connection.

The fluidity and diversity of love invite us to embrace the beauty found in the differences that define each love story. In acknowledging the uniqueness of individual narratives, in celebrating the richness of diverse expressions, and in actively participating in the ongoing evolution of love, we contribute to a tapestry that reflects the complexity, depth, and boundless possibilities inherent in modern relationships.

May the exploration of embracing the fluidity and diversity of love inspire individuals to approach relationships with openness, curiosity, and a commitment to fostering connections that honor the myriad ways in which love can be experienced and expressed. In doing so, we actively contribute to the ongoing narrative of love—a narrative that continues to unfold, evolve, and shape the very essence of human connection in the 21st century and beyond.

THE END

Glossary

Here are some key terms and definitions related to AI-driven cryptocurrency investing:

1. Modern Love: The contemporary expression of romantic relationships characterized by evolving dynamics influenced by societal changes and technological advancements.

2. Technological Influences: The impact of digital advancements on various aspects of modern romance, including communication, dating practices, and relationship dynamics.

3. Valentine's Day: An annual celebration of love and affection, often marked by the exchange of cards, gifts, and expressions of affection on February 14th.

4. Contemporary Dynamics: The current patterns and trends shaping the nature of love, relationships, and societal expectations in the present era.

5. Changing Perspectives: Evolving viewpoints and attitudes toward love, relationships, and the significance of traditional celebrations like Valentine's Day.

6. Dating Apps: Mobile applications designed to facilitate the initiation of romantic relationships by connecting individuals based on shared interests, preferences, or geographical proximity.

7. Online Communication: The use of digital platforms and tools for connecting and interacting with others, playing a significant role in modern relationship-building.

8. Virtual Connections: Relationships formed and maintained primarily through online platforms, transcending geographical limitations.

9. Social Media's Impact: The influence of social networking platforms on the dynamics of relationships, self-perception, and the public portrayal of romantic experiences.

10. Tech Innovations: Cutting-edge advancements that reshape traditional dating practices and introduce novel ways for individuals to connect and express romantic interest.

11. Evolving Notions: Changing concepts and ideas surrounding love, commitment, and partnership in response to societal shifts and individual preferences.

12. Shifting Gender Roles: Changes in societal expectations regarding the roles and responsibilities of individuals based on gender within romantic relationships.

13. Impact of Individualism: The influence of a cultural emphasis on personal autonomy and self-expression on the dynamics and expectations within partnerships.

14. Diversity in Relationships: The recognition and acceptance of various relationship structures and expressions beyond traditional norms.

15. Celebrity Influence: The effect of public figures and pop culture icons on shaping societal ideals and trends related to love and romantic gestures.

16. Virtual Celebrations: Commemorating special occasions, including Valentine's Day, through online platforms and shared digital experiences.

17. Long-Distance Love: Romantic relationships maintained over significant geographical distances, often facilitated by technology.

18. Psychosocial Perspectives: The psychological and societal viewpoints that influence individual behavior, emotions, and interactions within romantic relationships.

19. Globalization of Love: The interconnectedness of individuals from diverse cultural backgrounds, leading to cross-cultural relationships and international love.

20. Future Trends: Anticipated shifts and developments in the realm of love and relationships, often influenced by emerging technologies and changing societal norms.

Potential References

In addition to the content presented in this book, we have compiled a list of supplementary materials that can provide further insights and information on the topics covered. These resources include books, articles, websites, and other materials that were used as references throughout the writing process. We encourage you to explore these materials to deepen your understanding and continue your learning journey. Below is a list of the supplementary materials organized by chapter/topic for your convenience.

Introduction: Navigating Modern Love

Giddens, A. (1992). "The Transformation of Intimacy: Sexuality, Love, and Eroticism in Modern Societies." Stanford University Press.

Bauman, Z. (2003). "Liquid Love: On the Frailty of Human Bonds." Polity Press.

Chapter 1: Technological Influences on Modern Romance

Ellison, N. B., et al. (2014). "The role of relationships in the diffusion of information on social media sites: The case of Facebook relationship status updates." Journal of Computer-Mediated Communication, 19(3), 352-367.

Rosenfeld, M. J., & Thomas, R. J. (2012). "Searching for a mate: The rise of the internet as a social intermediary." American Sociological Review, 77(4), 523-547.

Chapter 2: Changing Dynamics of Romantic Relationships

Cherlin, A. J. (2004). "The deinstitutionalization of American marriage." Journal of Marriage and Family, 66(4), 848-861.

Schwartz, C. R., & Graf, N. L. (2009). "The impact of the transition to cohabitation on relationship quality: Testing the role of selectivity and timing." Social Science Research, 38(2), 229-244.

Chapter 3: Celebrity Influence on Valentine's Day Trends
Holmes, S. (2004). "Passions and constraints: On the theory of liberal democracy." University of Chicago Press.
Jerslev, A. (2016). "Celebrity and the media." Springer.
Chapter 4: Virtual Celebrations and Long-Distance Love
Ranzini, G., & Lutz, C. (2017). "Love at first swipe? Explaining Tinder self-presentation and motives." Mobile Media & Communication, 5(1), 80-101.
Stafford, L., & Merolla, A. J. (2007). "Idealization, reunions, and stability in long-distance dating relationships." Journal of Social and Personal Relationships, 24(1), 37-54.
Chapter 5: The Psychology of Love Today
Finkel, E. J., et al. (2014). "Online dating: A critical analysis from the perspective of psychological science." Psychological Science in the Public Interest, 13(1), 3-66.
Reis, H. T., & Aron, A. (2008). "Love: What is it, why does it matter, and how does it operate?" Perspectives on Psychological Science, 3(1), 80-86.
Chapter 6: Love in the Age of Globalization
Beck, U., & Beck-Gernsheim, E. (2014). "Distant Love: Personal Life in the Global Age." John Wiley & Sons.
Narayan, U. (1997). "Dislocating cultures: Identities, traditions, and Third World feminism." Routledge.
Chapter 7: Future Trends in Love and Relationships
Döring, N. (2017). "The Internet's impact on sexuality: A critical review of 15 years of research." Computers in Human Behavior, 76, 312-324.
Regan, P. C., & Dreyer, C. S. (1999). "Lust? Love? Status? Young adults' motives for engaging in casual sex." Journal of Psychology & Human Sexuality, 11(1), 1-24.
Conclusion: Love in the 21st Century

De Botton, A. (2006). "On Love." Grove Press.

Hendrick, C., & Hendrick, S. S. (2000). "Love and sex attitudes and practices in East Asia." Journal of Sex Research, 37(4), 321-327.

www.ingramcontent.com/pod-product-compliance
Lightning Source LLC
LaVergne TN
LVHW012044070526
838202LV00056B/5594